INTERNET MARKETING

THE KEY TO INCREASED HOME SALES

INTERNET MARKETING

THE KEY TO INCREASED HOME SALES

Mitch Levinson, MIRM, CSP

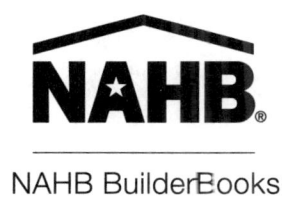

NAHB BuilderBooks

Internet Marketing: The Key to Increased Home Sales

BuilderBooks, a Service of the National Association of Home Builders

Elizabeth M. Rich	Director, Book Publishing
Natalie C. Holmes	Book Editor
Nevena Stankovic	Cover Design
Circle Graphics, Inc.	Composition
US Book Print Div. of Delta Graphic Mgmt., Inc.	Printing
Gerald M. Howard	NAHB Chief Executive Officer
Mark Pursell	NAHB Senior Vice President, Expositions, Marketing & Sales
Lakisha Campbell, CAE	NAHB Vice President, Publishing & Affinity Programs

Disclaimer

This publication provides accurate information on the subject matter covered. The publisher is selling it with the understanding that the publisher is not providing legal, accounting, or other professional service. If you need legal advice or other expert assistance, obtain the services of a qualified professional experienced in the subject matter involved. Reference herein to any specific commercial products, process, or service by trade name, trademark, manufacturer, or otherwise does not necessarily constitute or imply its endorsement, recommendation, or favored status by the National Association of Home Builders. The views and opinions of the author expressed in this publication do not necessarily state or reflect those of the National Association of Home Builders, and they shall not be used to advertise or endorse a product.

Printed in the United States of America

15 14 13 12   1 2 3 4 5

Library of Congress Cataloging-in-Publication Data

Levinson, Mitch, 1969-
  Internet marketing : the key to increased home sales / Mitch Levinson.
    p. cm.
  Includes bibliographical references and index.
  ISBN 978-0-86718-676-5 (alk. paper) -- ISBN 0-86718-676-3 (alk. paper) 1. Construction industry--
Marketing. 2. Real estate business--Marketing. 3. House selling. 4. Internet marketing. I. Title.
  HD9715.A2L435 2012
  333.33›830688--dc23

                        2011046267

For further information, please contact:

National Association of Home Builders
1201 15th Street, NW
Washington, DC 20005-2800
800-223-2665
Visit us online at www.BuilderBooks.com.

For my mom, who lost her battle with cancer as I was writing this book. She is the strongest person I have known. I love you Mom; this book is for you.

Contents

About the Author

Mitch Levinson, MIRM, CSP, is an Internet marketing expert who specializes in *search engine optimization (SEO)*, website development, e-mail marketing, social media, and customer relationship management (CRM) consulting services. He is known for creating effective programs that produce positive return on investment (ROI) by increasing traffic and sales, and generating revenue. Mitch is founder and president of MLC New Home Marketing and MLC Flat-Fee Realty, and managing partner of mRELEVANCE, LLC, an Internet marketing, social media, and public relations company with offices in Chicago and Atlanta.

Mitch is a multimillion dollar real estate sales producer. He has a BA from the University of Illinois and an MBA in computer information systems and e-commerce from Georgia State University. He brings a unique perspective and experience to the field of real estate communications, helping home builders and others gain a competitive advantage using new technology and the Internet to market and sell products and lifestyle. His home builder clients include large national public companies as well as small custom builders.

Prior to establishing MLC New Home Marketing, Mitch was the national builder consultant for MOVE.com, where he provided Internet, lead management and CRM solutions to help large national home builders sell homes more efficiently. When Move.com was originally launched as Homebuilder.com, Mitch was its first technical builder consultant and brought the first nine large national builders online with their *XML* listing data feeds. He also led the CRM and Internet marketing departments for Technical Olympic USA, a publicly traded company.

Mitch is an active broker in Illinois and Georgia and a member of the National Association of Home Builders (NAHB), Home Builders Association of Greater Chicago, Northern Illinois Home Builders Association, Southwest Suburban Home Builders Association, Greater Atlanta Home Builders Association, and the Atlanta Apartment Association. He is an NAHB Institute of Residential Marketing (IRM) trustee, a member of the National Sales and Marketing Council (NSMC) board, and serves on the Business Management and Information Technology Committee.

When he isn't behind a computer or on an iPhone, he enjoys participating in and watching sports, coaching his children's teams, and riding his motorcycle.

Acknowledgments

I want to thank everyone who has helped and encouraged me to write this book, as well as those who have participated in making me who I am today. My family is a central piece of my life and is the reason I work as hard as I do. Watching my three kids play sports and have fun gives me the energy to work hard and be the best person I can be. Helping them learn as they grow makes all the difference to them. Stacy, sometimes it's hard, but you are always there for me with whatever professional decisions I make. I would not have been able to write this book or be where I am today without you. For that I thank you. To my business partner, Carol, I learn from you every day and I love what we continue to build together. You rock, and what we do for our clients is awesome! To all my camping friends: I do not think I would have been able to finish this book if it were not for the Blackhawk crew. You guys are the best! To my Dad: thank you for pushing me as hard as you did to make me understand that effort and hard work lead to success, that it must come from within and it must be constant. And finally, Mom, you will always be my best friend and most important cheerleader. You were always there for me, and still are. Thank you for allowing me to be me.

Abbreviations

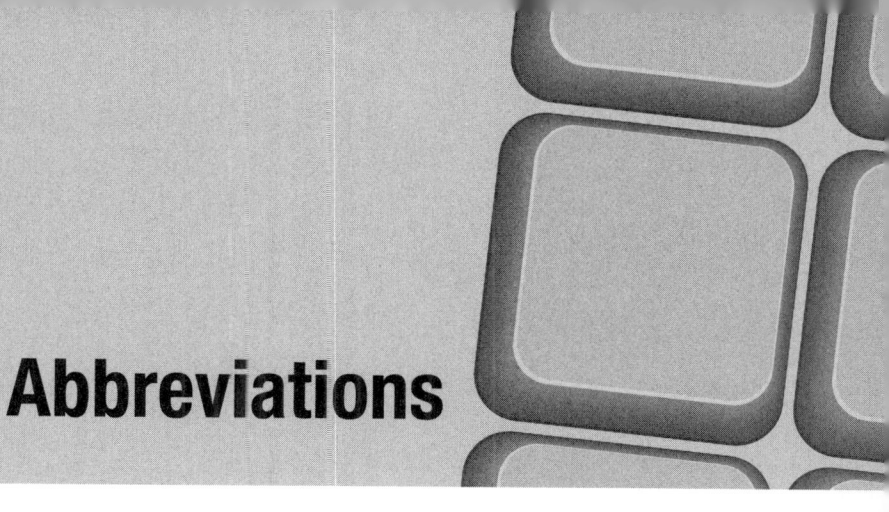

API	application programming interface
CMS	content management system
CPC	cost per click
CPM	cost per thousand
CRM	customer relationship management
DPI	dots per inch
HBA	home builders association
HTML	hypertext markup language
IRM	Institute of Residential Marketing
KPI	key performance indicator
MLS	Multiple Listing Service
NAHB	National Association of Home Builders
NAR	National Association of Realtors
NSMC	National Sales and Marketing Council
PAC	political action committee
PPC	pay per click
PR	page rank or public relations
ROI	return on investment
RSS	really simple syndication
SEM	search engine marketing
SEO	search engine optimization
SERP	search engine results page
SMO	social media optimization
WMT	webmaster tools
XML	extensible markup language

Introduction

I often hear home building industry professionals express frustration that using technology doesn't "come naturally" to them. Wii, iPhones, and Facebook were not around when they began their careers, let alone when they were in school. Although my career path might suggest otherwise, I also did not grow up immersed in technology the way most *Millennials* just entering the workforce now do. Computers were not standard equipment in real estate offices when I first became a Realtor in 1992.

If you have been "in the business" for some time, you may recall the early '90s housing market. Most real estate professionals, however, would prefer to forget it. Interest rates were more than 9%, which discouraged many would-be buyers. The Multiple Listing Service (MLS) published biweekly books of "current" active listings that were as thick as the *Yellow Pages*. Even though the content was stale and "new" listings were two weeks old when the book was printed and distributed, agents lugged these books around in our trunks or the backseats of our cars because we had no other option. We had to call each listing agent to find out whether a home was, in fact, still on the market, and stay abreast of market activity by driving around daily and noting "For Sale," "Under Contract," and "Sold" signs.

I used to create lists of homes I wanted to see and competitors I needed to shop. I was the new guy in the office then, learning from the seasoned veterans how to sell, where to stand, and what to ask. Then something happened. The MLS gave our office a computer so the service could send us a CD each week to replace the mammoth out-of-date books. Because I was more experienced with computers than my mentors, suddenly I was able to teach them something. I was not just the new guy anymore; I was the expert who could help them add their listings to the MLS and search for available homes to show their buyers. These are my good memories from the bad housing market of the early '90s, when I realized the power of technology to help people do their jobs more efficiently to reach their sales goals.

Times have changed and the role of technology continues to alter the home sales landscape. Although you still have to stay on top of the market by driving neighborhoods, listing data is readily available online, not just to you as a home sales professional but to your potential buyers as well. This makes your job a lot easier in some respects and much more challenging in others. The National Association of Realtors (NAR) says about 90% of home buyers use the Internet to look for a home.[1] Prospects conduct online research, create large lists of available homes, and begin to narrow their choices before you even know they are looking for a home. Although you may not have to spend time creating these lists for them, you need to make sure your homes stay on their list. So my job has changed. I still consider myself that "young kid" in the office (well, maybe not so young anymore) who helps others with technology, but it is more than that. I now help home sellers, including home builders, develop strategies to ensure they remain on the list of possibilities for prospects. Two decades after my first experience using computer technology to sell real estate, new technological tools available make the job more exciting today than it has ever been.

You can learn to use Internet marketing to sell more homes and increase your revenue starting today. I wrote this book not just to share my 20 years of experience, but to provide you with the know-how for using today's technology to keep your listings fresh, searchable, relevant, and at the top of homebuyers' lists. It shows you how to build the best websites, drive traffic to them, and engage buyers with them. The book will help you create and maintain your Internet marketing strategy confidently. You will learn to monitor how well your strategy is working and what you can do to improve your results. Whether you are a builder, developer, marketing specialist for new homes or the resale market, a trade contractor, trade association, materials supplier, or working in some other role in residential construction, or any industry for that matter, this book will help you work better and smarter. Each chapter is filled with specific ideas that you can use immediately and which will have a positive impact on your company.

How this Book is Organized

Each chapter provides an overview and detailed explanation of a particular facet of Internet marketing as well as specific techniques to apply the knowledge. The book includes real-world examples of effective Internet marketing and exercises, explains traps to avoid, provides step-by-step implementation strategies, offers connectivity and integration tips, and suggests budgeting strategies.

The real-world exercises are intended to help you learn from experience so you can understand specific concepts. Consider this your homework. Don't skip it! To improve your Internet marketing and communication, you must do your homework. I don't assign much, and what I assign is fun!

Connectivity

Connectivity and integration tips help you understand that a proper and effective marketing and communication strategy requires you to think about the big picture as you tie the individual components and tactics together. Building your program into an efficient machine with all the pieces working together will boost your competitive advantage. Pay close attention to connectivity; it will save time and increase efficiency.

Next Steps

Next steps are action items to help you understand what to do and the order for incorporating what you learn. People often ask me where to start or what to do next. This section will help you take that first or next step toward effective marketing.

Budget

Everything costs money. Even free websites require a time commitment for setup and maintenance. The Budget sections will help you estimate expenditures for a successful and effective program. Sometimes you will have to spend more than the suggested amount, and sometimes you can spend less. Use the guidelines provided to define your resource requirements realistically to achieve desired results.

Whether your goal is to become an expert or to better understand Internet marketing topics so you can better understand your web consultants, this book provides takeaways to move your marketing in new and exciting directions.

What is Internet Marketing?

The Internet has impacted nearly every aspect of our daily lives. It has changed how we work, shop, communicate and interact, conduct research, entertain, and educate ourselves. It also has changed how companies market products and services and build their brands. Anyone, anywhere, at any time can browse the web from a smart phone or tablet. Internet marketing uses the Internet to build a network to connect and communicate with your leads, prospects, and buyers as they research your products and make buying decisions. An effective Internet marketing strategy focuses on generating traffic and leads. Marketing 101 teaches that to be effective at reaching and engaging your target market, you need to be where the buyers are and present the right message to them. Those fundamental principles have not changed, but the Internet has created an opportunity to locate buyers more quickly. According to the World Bank, as of April 2011 almost 80% of the US population was online (up from 20% in 1997) (fig. 1.1).

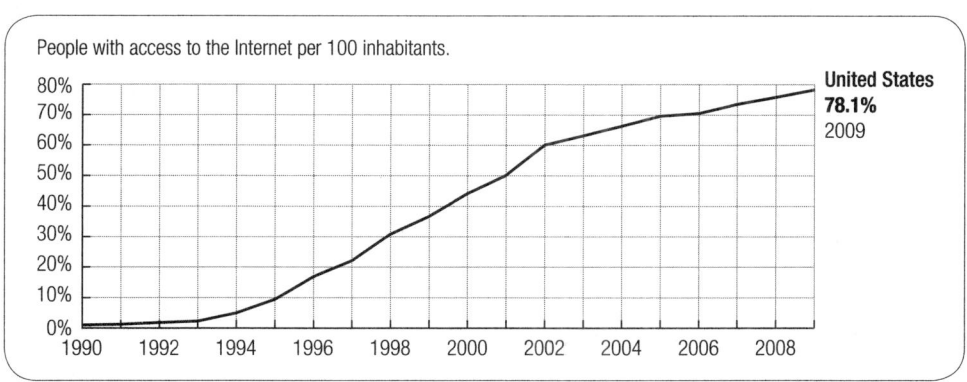

FIGURE 1.1 **World Internet Usage**
Internet use keeps growing. (Data source: World Bank, "World Development Indicators")

If you subtract the population of minors who are too young to buy and people who can't afford to buy a home, the statistics would be even more dramatic. In other words, nearly all of your prospects and buyers are online. If you want to be where your buyers are, secure a competitive advantage, and be effective in business (or even survive in business), you must embrace the Internet as mainstream and your "Main Street" for communicating with consumers. Successful companies in the home building industry, or any industry for that matter, have embraced the reality that people can access information about any company via the web anywhere and everywhere.

Internet marketing is not a fad; it is a marketing fundamental for successful companies that has been around for almost 20 years. If you are not ready and willing to learn how to market online, it may be time for you to retire to the country and build that dream home you always wanted. However, if you want to learn how to use the Internet and technology to stay competitive in a challenging and fast-paced market, keep reading.

Free Information: A Blessing and a Curse

Ready access to information about your business is both a blessing and a curse. Consumers can tell stories about your company—either positive or negative—to an audience of millions with a few keystrokes or the touch of their smartphone screen. Yes, you want your company's products and services to be well known, but you must ensure that they are known for the right reasons. Whether you want your products to be known for their uniqueness, reliability, or "coolness" factor, you want your target market to find this information and contact you to make a purchase.

The good news is you can use Internet marketing techniques to control messages about your company within this new media landscape and build your web presence to capture quality leads. Doing so will ensure that your intended message gets to consumers at the right time, in the right way, with the right call to action for them to connect with you.

Web 2.0

Web 2.0 is industry jargon for how people are using the Internet today to build websites, blogs, and social networking sites that encourage interaction and communication. Web 2.0 emphasizes information sharing, collaboration, communication, and interaction. Users find information easily, and can generate content and create virtual communities. In other words, Web 2.0 is the interactive and collaborative nature of websites, blogs, and social networking websites where web visitors can personally and directly interact with companies or other consumers. A user-friendly Web 2.0 website has the following attributes:

- Allows visitors to interact and collaborate
- Links to other websites
- Includes accessible interactive content about the company
- Promotes openness and transparency in buyer-company interaction

Creating a website, a blog, or both, for your company is a necessary step in Internet marketing. In fact, these components form the foundation of your program. But having a website, although necessary, is no longer sufficient. You need to be, and interact, on other Internet sites where your buyers get information, talk to friends, interact with coworkers, network, and have fun.

Strategy and Tactics

Strategy is the aerial view of all of the individual pieces and components of your Internet marketing program. Tactics are the ground-level components of your program and how you use them. Figure 1.2 illustrates an effective marketing strategy including specific tactics of a Web 2.0 marketing program. Just like any other area in your business, your marketing program begins with creating a written strategy that can be easily followed and improved upon along the way. Remember that your goal is to be where your target home buyers are and to stay on their list of possible builders for their next home. The best way to do this is to think first about your strategy and what its main component, or foundation, will be. Your website and blog are the foundation of your marketing strategy. Like a home's foundation, they must be strong enough to build your program on. The website and blog store valuable information about your company and deliver it to consumers. Whether you should have a website and a blog, a website that is a blog, or a blog within your website are questions answered in chapter 4. Your website/blog is the place to drive all traffic, especially prospects and buyers. There, you can manage your online content and ask for the sale. In a perfect world, you want all leads, prospects and buyers to come to your website. It is your virtual sales office and your most important sales person.

Your website is the single most important communication vehicle for your company and brand. It is also one of the few that you completely

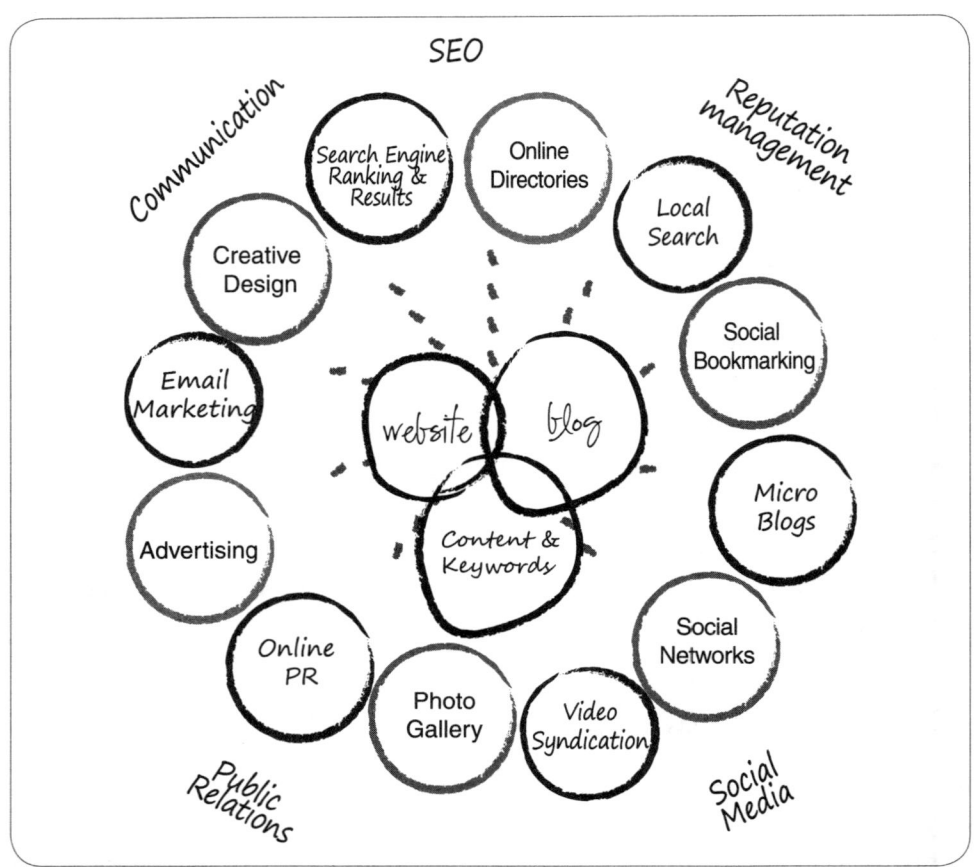

FIGURE 1.2 **Web 2.0 Marketing Plan**

Create a complete marketing program that integrates all marketing tactics with the blog and website as its foundation. (Source: mRELEVANCE, LLC)

control. You must take full advantage of your website by making it an effective tool to attract traffic and capture leads. After all, an effective marketing program will generate quality traffic and capture qualified leads. Your marketing program should

- drive traffic to your website;
- effectively convert web traffic to visitors to your sales center; and
- generate leads and prospects.

Your sales team will then take those potential home buyers and convert them into sales. Lead management is an essential component of your marketing program. Lead conversion is your primary source of revenue. Without a sound strategy and resources to follow up with leads to convert them into buyers, the website traffic you generate using the techniques explained in this book will be irrelevant.

Each element of your strategy must work effectively with and reinforce the others. You must design and build your website so both consumers and the search engines can find it. You need a strong search engine optimization (SEO) and social media marketing program with the right *keywords*. You must include blogging, online public relations, social networking, and social bookmarking in your tactics. Ensure local search sites include positive information and recommendations for your company. You need to be everywhere home buyers might be and provide opportunities for your marketing team to communicate regularly and directly with these leads and prospects by e-mail, text messages, and through social networks. Position advertising, whether online or elsewhere, to attract attention and include a call to action consumers will respond to. Finally, include tracking devices for determining what works and what doesn't so you can adjust your strategy to be more effective.

Keywords and Strategy

A sound Internet marketing strategy begins with goals, and then develops tactics and allocates or aligns resources to accomplish specific objectives. A holistic marketing plan details specific tactics and action items that will help achieve the goals. For example, to achieve the goal of driving quality traffic to your website, you must identify and use targeted keywords and keyword phrases. These are the words, in a specific order, you think quality home prospects will type in the search box on the search engines when they are exploring a home purchase. For example, if you build new homes in Raleigh, you may think that someone who is considering purchasing a home in Raleigh will type "new homes in Raleigh" in Google to find their next home. The words "Raleigh new homes" might also be a keyword phrase you would want to target. Think about what terms a person would search if they didn't know the name of your company but were looking for the type of home you build, community you develop, or location where you sell homes. Would they search for "green homes" or for homes in a specific area of town?

Your marketing strategy must carefully consider both the vocabulary that will deliver the right message to your website visitors and the words the search engines will look for to rank your site's relevance when users type in a search term. There is an art and science to selecting and using the right keywords. Picking keywords is half the battle; the other half is using them the right way.

Two Types of Traffic

There are two types of Internet traffic you want to attract to your website: consumer traffic and *search engine traffic.* Consumer traffic is website visitors. You can measure it in numbers. People come to your site because they know who you are, or they get to your site through a link from another site, or by typing a keyword in a search engine and clicking on your site in the list of results. Search engine traffic is just that—traffic from the tools that the search engines use to rank your site in their results pages. It can be quantified by how often you can get the search engines to come to your site, read the content on your site, index each page, and rank your site based on its relevance to specific keywords. The keywords you choose will directly impact both kinds of traffic. In fact, every component of your marketing plan will use your targeted keywords. The right words used the right way will attract the right traffic.

The quality of consumer or home buyer traffic is a *key performance indicator (KPI)* to track and benchmark each month. You want to increase the number of people who visit your website, especially if they are in the market to purchase a new home. If improving the amount of traffic to your website is good; then improving the quality of that traffic is even better. That is why selecting the right keywords is critical to your marketing program. It is also why search engine traffic is even more important than consumers, buyers, and their eyeballs. Search engine traffic is more important than consumer traffic because it creates even more consumer traffic

Search engines read the content on a website to determine its relevance to a given search term and topic. The more relevant the site is to word phrases, the higher that site appears on a *search engine results page (SERP)* and the more searches the site appears in. For example, Google has software programs, called *bots* or *spiders,* which are designed to surf the web and index every page and every link on every page online. These spiders crawl from page to page, reading the content, identifying relevant keywords and clicking on every link. They index every page of relevant content and associate the page with relevant words. This is how Google determines the list of results for each search term. Through a complex *algorithm,* a mathematical formula based on several private and undocumented variables, Google and the other search engines determine the order in which websites are listed in the SERPs. For your site to rank high, you need to get the bots to: 1) visit your site quickly, 2) return often, and 3) index your site and its content for the relevant words you are targeting.

Because there are many bots and several computers indexing the Internet simultaneously, people searching the Internet in different locations at different times may see a different set of results using the same keywords. To understand this better, assume Google had to explore the entire United States and draw a map of all the streets and waterways using four groups of explorers. If one group started in Maine, one in Florida, one in California, and one in Washington state, and they drove each road and paddled every waterway while mapping their findings, each group would have a different set of results at any given time. Even if their territories overlapped, when a new street was built after one of the explorers passed by, only the next one to pass by would see it so only the second explorer would have that street on his or her map. Although the *Googlebot* technology is more efficient than what the early explorers like Lewis and Clark had, it may take up to 24 hours for new websites to propagate through the Internet and the search engines to locate them.

After the bots finish compiling an index for a search, they start the process all over again. When you continually feed the search engines new content, they will return to your site for more. And if Google visits your site often and considers it relevant for your targeted keywords, your site will be indexed higher than other sites. The higher your site is ranked for your targeted keywords and the more times your website appears in a SERP, the more quality consumer eyeballs you will get.

Marketing 101

In general, when you adapt traditional marketing concepts to new Internet marketing techniques, you will produce an effective strategy. By combining your SEO and online presence with traditional marketing tactics, like branding your company and product(s), incorporating creative, designing eye-catching marketing collateral, running effective campaigns, and defining and delivering your message effectively, you will increase sales at a fraction of the cost of other marketing methods. For example, a home builder client in Lakeland, Florida, reduced its advertising budget by 75% between 2008 and 2011 but nearly doubled contracts. Website and blog traffic more than doubled–from some 3,400 visitors in August 2008 to nearly 8,700 visitors in January 2011.

The Four Ps

When you apply the *Four Ps* of marketing to your Internet marketing program, you create an effective marketing strategy. The Four P's of Marketing are:

1. **Product**–the tangible goods or services you offer as a builder, remodeler, or other business. For example, the house and physical structure, the features, the craftsmanship, the appliances, the community amenities, and all the items that go into what is offered and available for a home and within a community make up the product. Keep in mind that even the best marketing or advertising campaign will not sell a bad product.
2. **Price**–the decisions that affect how much you charge for and what a buyer may be willing to pay for the product. Base price, how to package options, and whether to include a lot or offer it separately are a few components of pricing decisions. Market research and the *absorption* of your homes indicate whether your product is priced correctly for the market. Even if you build a great home, if the price is too high for your market, if the market is saturated, or if demand is limited, you will have trouble selling it.
3. **Place**–the location of your community or house and where housing consumers can go to purchase your home(s). Do you have a sales center in a model home, trailer, or in a strip mall? Is your website a virtual storefront that encourages consumers to contact you, displays product options, and helps you sell your homes? These are place-based questions.
4. **Promotion**–all of the communication tools that a marketer uses to publicize a product. Advertising, public relations, and sales are three components of promotion. This book will help you to think outside these boxes and incorporate new promotional tools in your marketing strategy. An effective strategy goes way beyond advertising your homes and communities.

An effective Internet marketing program will build on these four concepts, and add a fifth–people–to the marketing mix. People–your sales and marketing team members—are your front line. They are the representatives buyers interact with when they are on your website, Facebook page, or Twitter. They are your ambassadors for the company. When you successfully incorporate your team members into your marketing mix, they will exponentially enhance your promotional efforts.

Internet Marketing Toolbox

Your Internet marketing toolbox includes your website and blog (the foundation) and micro-blogs, social networks, online public relations, local search sites, e-mail marketing, Internet advertising, lead management, and tracking analytics. I have been accused of thinking more like a search engine than a person when I consider marketing goals, strategies, and tactics, and I do consider search engine optimization to be a critical tactic for an Internet marketing program. After reading this book, you will be able to use these tools in your business to become a more effective Internet marketer.

Internet Marketing Toolbox

- Website and/or blog
- Keyword strategy
- SEO
- Microblogs
- Social networks
- Local search sites
- Online PR
- Photo sharing
- Video syndication
- Social bookmarking
- Search marketing
- Internet advertising
- Lead management
- CRM
- E-mail marketing
- Website tracking
- Search engine rank tracking

Design
opment

Your company website is your main channel and your most important vehicle for enhancing your company image, building your brand, and showcasing your products. It is also the most appropriate place to communicate with your customers. But before you rebuild your website or start any Internet marketing project, you need a plan.

Just as clear goals are essential to developing a business plan and an effective marketing strategy, creating specific goals for your website to accomplish is central to creating a powerful site. With clearly written and realistic goals for your website, you will be able to assess its effectiveness after launch. A specific goal for your website can be "to drive three additional traffic units to my sales center each month" or "increase website traffic by 30% over three months." Whatever your goals are, clearly define and prioritize them at the start of your project so you'll be able to assess your website's effectiveness, using key performance indicators (KPIs), and make changes that will improve your results.

Goal Setting Exercise

Goals must be specific, timely, tangible, and realistic. You also have to write them down and look at them regularly in order to take daily steps toward achieving them. Each goal should increase the interaction of consumers with your website or drive traffic to your sales center. Include a numerical measurement for each goal and a deadline for seeing the desired results. Be very careful to only set goals for which you can accurately measure performance. You must be able to track progress and report results. Don't rely exclusively on your on-site sales team asking visitors how they heard about your company. Instead, look at your website tracking to see where your visitors come from or the names you get from your website or calls. Avoid setting unrealistic and unattainable goals or goals that are simply too easy to attain. You want to create goals that will really mean something when you achieve them. Take out a sheet of paper or open a new word document and complete the exercise below:

1. Write three goals you want your website to accomplish in the next 90 days.
2. Write three goals you want your website to accomplish in the next 6 months.
3. Write three goals you want your website to accomplish in the next 2 years.

Revisit these goals regularly and take steps each day to achieve them.

From Online to On-site

Consumers research and make preliminary decisions about homes, builders, and real estate professionals based on what they find on the Internet. They use the Internet to create a list of possible home builders. Of course, prospective home buyers will want to see the craftsmanship and construction quality of a home, speak with a salesperson about features and community amenities, and talk about mortgage and financing options before they make a purchase decision. Your Internet marketing campaign is designed to improve your search engine results, but driving traffic from the Internet to your home sales center is the ultimate goal of improving your online visibility. Therefore, you must get online visitors so excited about what they see that they will hop in their car and drive to your sales center. Your main goal for your website is to get a web visitor to contact your salespeople and experience your product. Because they can't touch and feel your product on the Internet, the challenge is to rapidly differentiate yourself and your homes from your competitors'. You want to stay on the prospects' list of builders to contact and models to see.

With 24/7 access to online information about homes, communities, and builders, consumers can quickly create a list of builders and homes they want to see. When the list becomes too long and contains too many homes, they simply shorten their list based on location,

Take a quick look back at the goals you created in the last section. Are there some goals that focus on getting buyers to visit your sales center and experience your product? If not, go back now and make adjustments. The point of the goal-setting exercise is to get the goals right so you can use them to build your business.

home styles, price range, and builder. They begin to eliminate builders and homes from the list to make it more manageable.

Five Website Features

Having an effective website can ensure that your company makes a consumer's short list. Your website should include the following five elements:

1. Rich and relevant content
2. *Intuitive* navigation
3. Attractive design
4. Functionality (the "coolness" factor)
5. Effectiveness in converting traffic to visitors

Rich and Relevant Content

Before deciding what information about your homes and communities to include on your website, take a step back and think like a home buyer. You want to give your web visitor the information they need to decide to contact you. If you were a home buyer, what would you look for on a website about homes? What would you want to find?

Buyers need to find the information they are interested in, not what you want to tell them. Unlike when print display and classified ads dominated the market and the goal was to provide "just enough" information to get prospects to contact you, buyers now get frustrated very easily and quickly if they can't find what they want immediately. They will abandon your website in a hurry if you don't provide useful information. Your job is to maintain consumers' interest in your site, keep them there longer exploring your products, and encourage them to take action.

Provide your company contact information on every page. You can't assume visitors will look hard to find a way to contact you or even click your "Contact Us" button. In addition, because buyers seek instant gratification and reasons to eliminate you from their long list of options, you must provide information to persuade them to come to your sales center. Give your buyers what they want. Display home prices, floor plans, square footage, features, and amenities. Home buyers must be able to get to your list of products and pricing for each base plan or inventory home as quickly as possible—within two to three clicks at most.

Acadia Homes organizes important product information on a clean, uncluttered page so visitors can easily find what they are looking for (fig. 2.1). Notice how you are drawn to the image of the community amenities, but you can easily find the key community information on the right, the list of plans and available inventory on the bottom, and the call to action ("Schedule an Appointment") in the middle of the page.

The more useful information you provide, the longer website visitors will stay on your site and explore your products. *Stickiness* is the term used to describe the amount of time a visitor will stay on your site. Stickiness is a

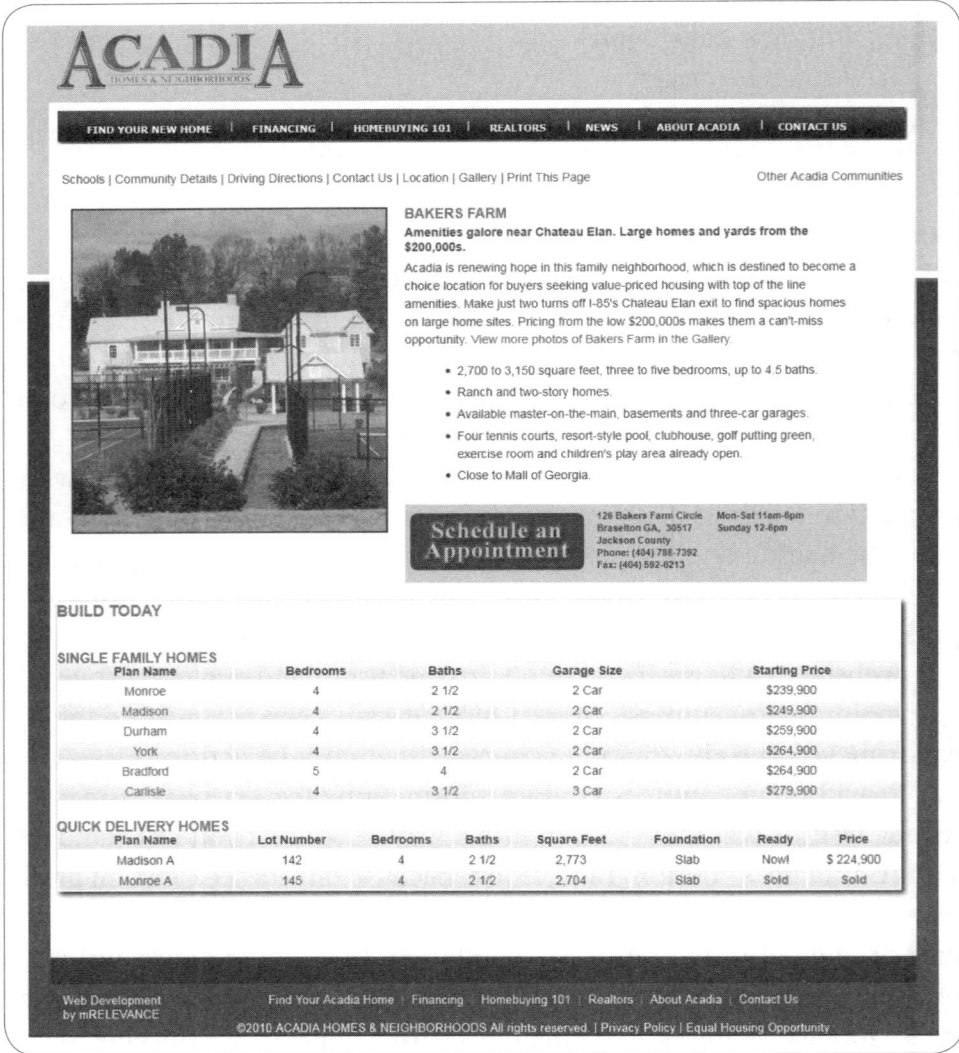

FIGURE 2.1   **Acadia Homes Community Page**

This clean-looking web page places information at the user's fingertips and features an effective call to action in a prominent location. (Reprinted with permission from Acadia Homes, Atlanta, Georgia)

good indicator for evaluating the quality of your online content. In addition to keeping them on your site longer, providing useful information allows them to self-qualify, which can make your sales process more efficient. When a customer enters the sales center and they already know which plan they like and can afford, your sales team can move ahead to discuss features and benefits and generally work smarter with each buyer.

In fact, your sales associates should consider web visitors to your sales center return visitors ("be-backs") because they already have seen and read about your homes and are ready to tour a model, if you have one. They may even know more about your company, your homes and your competitors than your sales team. Because these visitors already have decided they liked your product enough to take action by visiting, your sales team can work to build the relationship necessary to close on a home.

Providing comprehensive information on your website also enhances your company's reputation. Consumers today look for transparency in sales transactions. They already have a wealth of information at their fingertips. They are rightfully suspicious when information that should be accessible is not. If you require visitors to log in before providing access to pricing information or images of your floor plans, consumers may believe you are trying to hide something, that your company is sneaky or, even worse, that your company is in trouble. They may believe the stale content on your website reflects your company's building practices or viability. Their path of least resistance then is to just cross you off their list and visit your competitors.

Content Essentials

Home buyers are looking for basic introductory information about your homes, details about your communities, and information about your company. They care about the lifestyle your homes will offer them, so make sure content that describes features and amenities, and the builder story, demonstrate how your homes will suit a particular lifestyle. Use sentences and bullets. Don't use acronyms and industry jargon. Your website content must include the following items:

- Product and pricing, including base price and inventory homes
- Floor plans and images
- Elevation options
- Square footage
- Maps and locations with driving directions or a link to a map with directions

- Features and amenities
- Contact information, including company address and phone number
- Links to social media sites and online profiles
- Builder or company story

When you write content for each of these areas, use keywords your buyers will type into the search engines to conduct their searches. Describe features and amenities using terms consumers understand, not industry terminology. Consumers must be able to easily understand the content and quickly find the keywords that are important to them. As you will learn in chapter 3, you want your content to be well written for consumers, and also relevant for the search engines.

Figures 2.2 and 2.3 show two effective examples of builder websites that have provided relevant content and information, written for both home buyers and search engines. Sterling Custom Homes and Boone Homes build different products in different markets, and have different brand messages. But home buyers have positive experiences on either of these sites. The Sterling Custom Homes website compartmentalizes information on the home page to draw web visitors into the site and enable them to get the information they want quickly. The Boone Homes site displays the company's community and products in a format that is clean and easy to read.

Intuitive Navigation

One consequence of the instant-gratification information age we live in is that consumers have short attention spans and are impatient online. Your website visitors better be able to find whatever they are looking for after two to three clicks or they may become frustrated and go elsewhere to find it. Fortunately, you can build your website to be intuitive, to lead your visitor through your site creatively, so he or she doesn't need to rely on arrows and previous/next buttons to move through it. Build your site and your navigation logically from your visitor's perspective. Make it easy for them to get where they are going. This will keep visitors on your site longer and help your website achieve its goals.

Consider both available space and its location when you design your website. Website users typically scan content in an F-shaped pattern.[2] Our eyes intuitively look top and left first, and then sweep left to right across

FIGURE 2.2

Figure 2.2 Sterling Custom Homes Home Page

This web page helps users find information and navigate easily through the website. (Reprinted with permission from Sterling Custom Homes, Austin, Texas)

FIGURE 2.3

Boone Homes Community Page

The page looks and feels clean and still offers comprehensive information with an effective call to action. (Reprinted with permission from Boone Homes, Richmond, Virginia)

the dominant elements on a page. Next, our eyes scan from top to bottom on the left side, and finally across the middle of the page to the right. This is why web developers generally design page templates with the company name and logo in the left corner and primary navigation, or top-level navigation, at the top or left. Other content typically populates the middle and right. Think through each page during design to confirm that the design considers intuitive navigation.

Your top-level navigation—the menu of links to the main areas or sections of your website—should be across the top or down the left side. Try to limit the top-level navigation items to seven or fewer. Giving visitors too many choices at this level will overwhelm them with information and your page will look crowded and confusing. Limit the headings of the section or labels of your navigation to one or two words to facilitate rapid scanning. Because you only have a few clicks to work with, you must make your navigation intuitive. Following are recommendations for keeping your navigation simple and intuitive:

- Consider web page "real estate," and then put the most important items in the most important places according to the F pattern.
- Place your company name and logo in the top left corner.
- Put primary *navigation bars* (menus) at the top or left side of pages.
- Confine navigation menus to seven or fewer primary items.
- Limit menu headings to one or two words.
- Maintain only one or, at most, two levels of navigation. More than that will overwhelm and confuse your visitor.

Gerstad Builders (fig. 2.4) and Rockledge Apartments (fig. 2.5) have created easy and intuitive web navigation. Look at the prime real estate on their sites and what your eyes are drawn to. Gerstad Builders draws your attention to the company logo, its communities, and community map. Rockledge Apartments highlights the company's logo, phone number and its apartments. You can see in these examples that you know where to click next to get what you want.

Scavenger Hunt Usability Study

My barometer for the *usability,* the appearance of and navigability of websites my company launches was my mom. I would e-mail a link to

FIGURE 2.4 Gerstad Builders Home Page

Notice how communities are the focal point of the page. (Reprinted with permission from Gerstad Builders, McHenry, Illinois)

her for the site and she would try to navigate it. Like any good mother, she would always provide constructive feedback and wouldn't hesitate to tell me if there was something wrong or if she had trouble finding specific information. Here's another effective and inexpensive way to assess the navigability of your website:

1. Choose 10–15 facts on your website (e.g., specific home plans or prices, your preferred lender, year the company was founded).
2. Create a list of questions based on these facts (e.g., "What 4 bedroom home with a master bedroom on the main level

FIGURE 2.5

Rockledge Home Page

Notice how the logo and phone number attract your attention. (Reprinted with permission from Ceebraid Signal, Stamford, Connecticut)

could I build in Westgate?" or "When was the company founded?").

3. Enlist a group of friends, school-aged children of employees, existing home owners, or a combination of all three to find the answers on your website.

4. Ask each person to note the answers and how long it took to find them.

This type of usability study should be done regularly on your website, and especially after you launch a new one. Getting as much feedback as possible about how easy or difficult it is to navigate will help you enhance the user experience. Many people may want to be nice, rather than honest, if they find your site hard to navigate. Ask them to be critical, and make sure everyone who reviews the site provides at least one comment or suggestion.

Attractive Design

The Internet is a visual medium so the better your site looks, the better your company looks. Your website can follow all of the steps to being intuitive to navigate and still not be effective because it is boring. Like so many other tools in your Internet marketing toolbox, website design is a delicate balance of art and science, of flash and functionality. Design, in this context, refers to the outward appearance of a website, its creative layout and how the images, words and links display on the page. You probably have gone to a website looking for specific information like a business's location, hours, or product pricing, only to encounter a *landing page* with a 30-second video you had to watch first. Man, that was frustrating. Usually it takes me about 5 seconds to find the "stop" or "skip" button before I abandon the page.

Design is all about balance. Making your website fun and interactive, with movement and advanced interactive capabilities like video and motion, can really enhance the visitor experience. However, not providing your visitor an easy way to avoid these bells and whistles may be a turnoff that discourages them from returning. Your website should be interactive and not interrupt your buyer's search for information. Moreover, some enhancements will interfere with your SEO efforts. For example, a website that uses *Adobe Flash,* a cool tool that graphic designers and web developers use to simulate motion on a website, is difficult for Google to read and index, and most smartphone web browsers cannot view Flash. If your website doesn't enhance your company's search engine results or ignores the drastically increasing number of Internet users who browse the web using smartphones, it cannot be an effective marketing tool. Using motion in small doses will enhance your web presence, but make sure your site can be read and indexed in the search engines so that potential home buyers will find your company. Once web visitors find your site, its design either reinforces or detracts from your brand; it is never neutral.

Although you may incorporate full-motion video or another Flash element (such as an interactive floor plan) as a component of your website, don't make a Flash page your landing page. Instead, place Flash elements elsewhere and link to them from one of your web pages. Your visitors can decide whether to look at them. If you use video, it should be clear, relevant to the topic of the web page, and accompany other content (not stand alone on its own page).

Like Flash and movement, music and sound usually are not appropriate features for a website outside of the entertainment or gaming industries. In isolated circumstances, like the background music for a video or slide show, or a voice-over narration describing a section of the website, music and sound can be effective. However, unless you ask the visitor first if they want to experience your website with the music or video, it is a good idea to leave it out for these three reasons: 1) Your musical taste will differ from that of at least some visitors and you don't want them to form an opinion about you because of it; 2) Music will slow the performance of your website, including page loading; and 3) Users don't like unexpectedly encountering sound on a website, especially if they are trying to surf the Internet discreetly. (Most web surfing occurs Monday through Friday during business hours.)

The Connecticut's Best Apartments website (http://www.ctbestapts.com) illustrates effective use of Flash. Notice how the interactive map scrolls out from the top right (fig. 2.6). Fig. 2.7 demonstrates some mouse-over effects on the map. The map and header area are Flash components of the website. They are simple, clean and still easy navigate. Best of all, the search engines are still able to read and index their keyword-rich content below the map.

Sights and Sounds

- Full Flash websites may look cool, but the search engines can't read their content and indexing them for their relevant targeted keywords is a struggle.
- Music and sound are distracting. If you use them, do so sparingly, and offer options to turn them off.

 Connecticut's Best Apartments Home Page
Home page with the Flash map hidden. (Reprinted with permission from Ceebraid Signal, Stamford, Connecticut)

Functionality: The "Coolness" Factor

Beyond video and Flash, you have many options for building advanced features into your website to make it interactive. Having a "cool" website that uses the latest technology shows you are on the cutting edge of the industry and tells your website visitors that your company stays on top of current building trends. The "cooler" your website, the more credible you appear. The more credible you are, the better they think you build. It shows pride in workmanship and indicates your company's superiority. It gives you a competitive advantage over the company that builds across the street because buyers become interested enough to drive out to see you (and pass by all those other builders along the way.) On the other hand, a stale website reduces your company's chances to convert web visitors

 FIGURE 2.7 **Connecticut's Best Apartments Home Page with Flash**
Home page with the Flash map displayed. (Reprinted with permission from Ceebraid Signal, Stamford, Connecticut)

into sales, will have a negative impact on your brand, and may even give your prospects reason to believe you are out of business. So keep your site fresh and cool.

Following are some options for incorporating cool advanced functionality into your website:

- **Google Maps.** You can show visitors your exact location, and the mouse-over pop-up window can include pictures, headlines, content and links. Google Maps can also include driving directions from any location, show different map "views" (satellite view or street, for instance), and display other points of interest through Google Places. Google maps has an *application programming interface (API),* a set of instructions and routines that allows web developers to integrate specific functionality into a website so a map can display on your website several different ways. If you want a unique custom background, however, Google Maps may not be for you. Also, avoid displaying too much location information on your map. The goal is to get home buyers to your community, not all over town. Figure 2.8 shows an effective use of a Google Map.

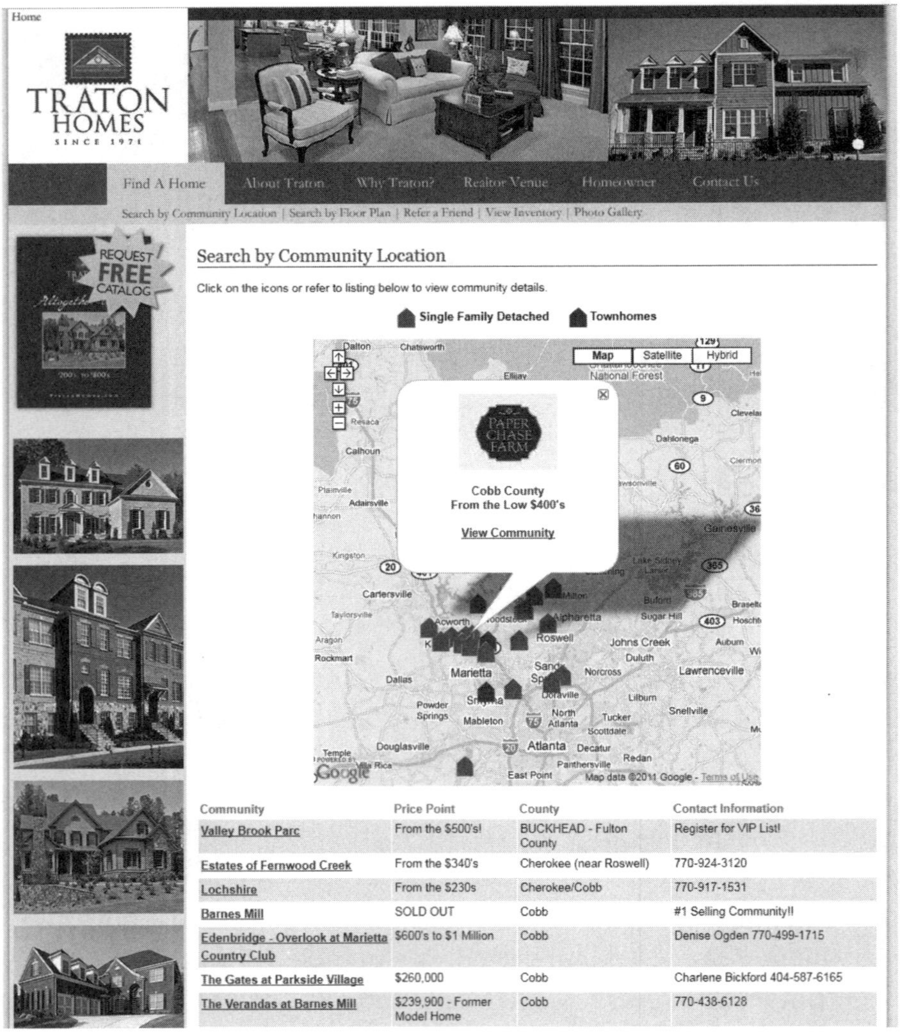

FIGURE 2.8 Traton Homes Map Page

Notice how the map shows the communities and references other locations. (Reprinted with permission from Traton Homes, Marietta, Georgia)

- **Interactive floor plans.** In contrast to static floor plans, these plans allow your website visitors to see pictures or images of specific components of your homes, and how various options will impact a home design, helping them visualize living in your home. I recommend hiring a company, possibly the one that creates your renderings and floor plan brochures, to create interactive floor plans for your website. The interactive features should be easy to use. For example, users should be able to check a box to add a fireplace or convert a loft into a fourth bedroom. Other types of interactive floor plans allow users to place an image on a floor plan simply by hovering their mouse pointer in a particular location (fig. 2.9). Companies that create interactive floor plans are listed in the Resources at the back of the book.
- **Interactive site map.** This type of map shows visitors the status of each lot in your community in real time. When your website is integrated with other company software, like the customer relationship management (CRM) system your sales team uses to write contracts or your production software that helps your team manage lot and scheduling information, you can display real-time information. This information may include lot availability, plan fit requirements, pricing, and other lot features. Having this visual online also empowers your sales team to work smarter. Team members can see on their desktops exactly what properties are available at a given time. Fig. 2.10 shows an effective site map.
- **Advanced listing and community search.** These two functions can automatically adjust the inventory a website visitor will see based on his or her selections, such as plan, price, and location. If you have a database that stores your communities and listings, you have many options for adding these two features. It is worth your time and effort to set up many different ways for home buyers to search because you want people to be able to self qualify before visiting your community. Two great examples of home and model searches are on the Acadia Homes (fig. 2.11) and Highland Homes (fig. 2.12) websites. Notice how Acadia Homes has the search criteria on the left side, and the results filter when a user clicks to modify the search criteria. Highland Homes uses different types of search criteria input. Your site may use *pull-down choices, checkboxes, radio buttons* or other types of input fields on the advanced listing or community search.

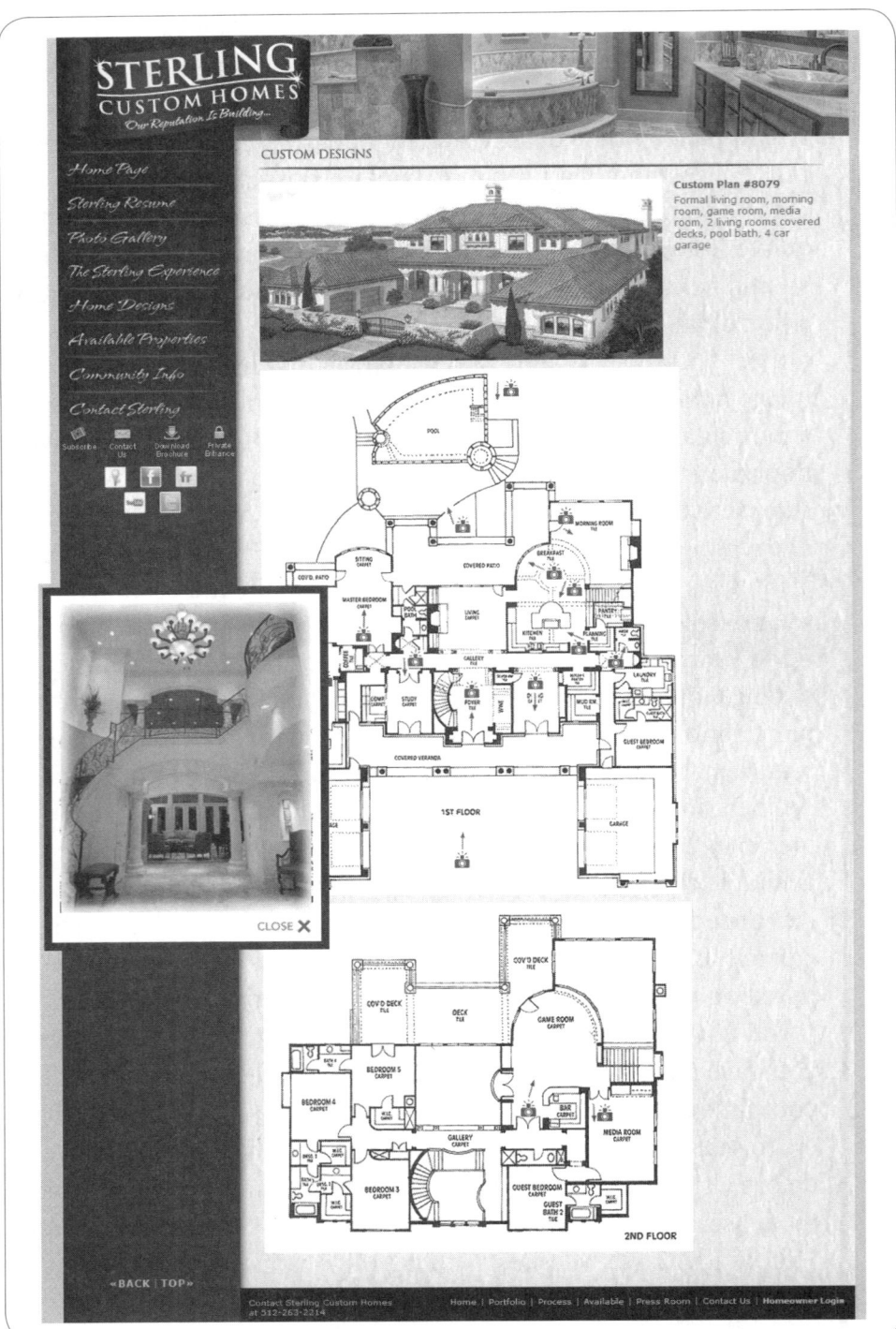

<table>
<tr><td>FIGURE
2.9</td><td>

Sterling Custom Homes Interactive Floor Plan

A photo displays when a user hovers the mouse pointer over a location on the floor plan.
(Reprinted with permission from Sterling Custom Homes, Austin, Texas)</td></tr>
</table>

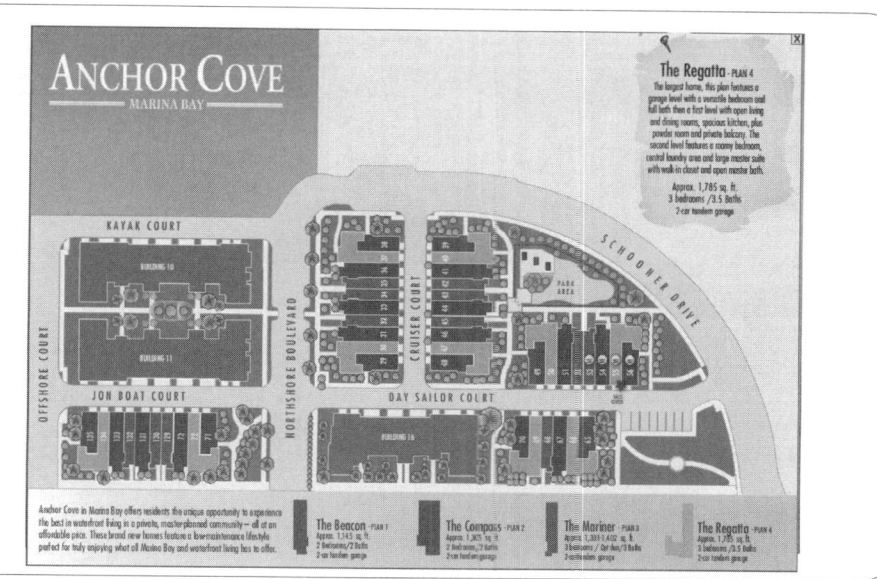

 Figure 2.10 Signature Homes Site Plan
Signature Homes shows which properties are available on its website. (Reprinted with permission from Signature Homes, Pleasanton, California)

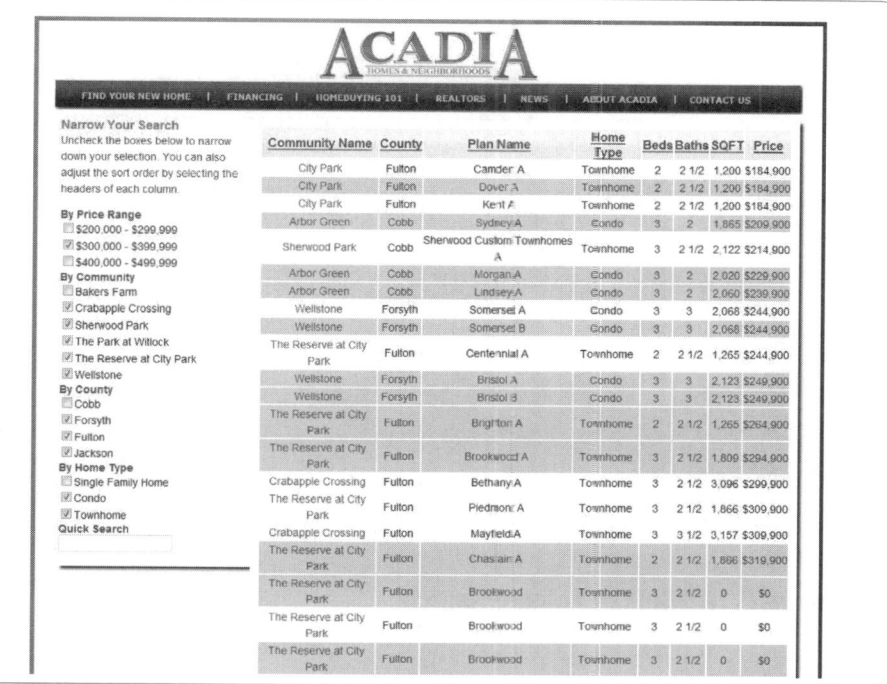

Figure 2.11 Acadia Home Search
The search filters appear on the left side. (Reprinted with permission from Acadia Homes, Atlanta, Georgia)

FIGURE 2.12

Figure 2.12 Highland Model Search

The search filters appear at the top of the list. (Reprinted with permission from Highland Homes, Lakeland, Florida)

- **Live help and chat.** Live online help and chat give your visitors immediate access to a sales counselor and a way to capture leads online. Although some software for help and chat can be easy to install and inexpensive, obviously live help and chat functionality requires a staff person to monitor and respond to requests. My six favorite chat software choices are listed in the Resources at the back of the book.

- **Photo galleries.** The Internet is a visual medium. High-quality pictures of your homes and photo galleries that display the product, lifestyle, events, and amenities are essential to every home builder's website. These photos should help visitors see themselves living in your homes and visualize enjoying your community's amenities. Following are guidelines for gathering and uploading photos to your website:

  - **Don't ask a sales associate to photograph** your homes and communities or try to do it yourself. This is one of the most common marketing mistakes home builders make. Because showing off your homes and communities is so central to your website marketing, you should hire a professional photographer. Pictures of your homes cannot be "good enough" for your website; they have to be great! A professional will ensure the right composition, lighting, and colors. Depending on his or her reputation, clientele, and the market, a professional photographer may charge hundreds or thousands of dollars for a daylong photo shoot. Consider this money well spent and a resource that you can use across several of the Internet marketing tools in your toolbox.

  - **Follow copyright rules and regulations.** You cannot "borrow" an image simply because it is online even if it is on a photo sharing site. Photographers own the rights to their photos. That means you need specific written permission and license to use an image. Copyright infringement penalties are steep. They can be $10,000 per occurrence. There are plenty of inexpensive photo sites where you can purchase and license stock photos to be used as lifestyle images on your website. My three favorites are www.istockphoto.com, www.punchstockphoto.com, and www.shutterstock.com, but you can always Google "stock photo sites" to find others. Images are offered in various sizes and price ranges.

Image Resolution

High-resolution images are painfully slow to load for most users, so you should only use low-resolution images on your website. Have your photographer save high-resolution images for your printed marketing collateral and low-resolution images for your website.

If I am planning to use an image only for the website, I usually purchase a low-resolution (72 *dpi*) image and a single-usage license for less than $10; if I want to use an image for a printed piece, all I need to do is upgrade my purchase, pay a little more, and download the same image at a higher resolution. High resolution and additional-use licenses can cost a few to a few hundred dollars more. Whichever site you use, review the license so that you understand the usage restrictions.

- Make sure your photographer delivers your photos in one of these three preferred formats: JPG, PNG, or GIF. These are common formats every photographer is familiar with.

- **Videos.** If a picture is worth a thousand words, then effectively placed videos may be worth a million. Use them to enhance written descriptions and other static website content to make your site more interactive and entertaining. Video can help describe your product, showcase your community amenities, detail your construction process, offer testimonials in your customer's own words, and tell your company's story. You can also *syndicate* them to drive traffic and capture leads. With the existence of YouTube and video-sharing sites like it, Internet users are more apt to trust videos that appear homegrown or even spontaneous. For example, 60–90-second videos of your current home owners giving a testimonial about your company and the excellent experience they had purchasing and building one of your homes are assets to your website. Some types of videos, however, should be planned and probably require a script and even a *story board*. Videos about a particular plan or move-in ready inventory home should be planned, rather than spontaneous. Unlike still photos, your sales team may be able to shoot both kinds of video. They will need a tripod (to reduce shaking) and probably an external microphone, but you can get a good Internet-ready video camera for $100–$200. Make sure there is a well-written script and that subjects practice what they plan to say on a video.

Consider hiring a professional to shoot video that will be a centerpiece of your home page or marketing campaign. Highlighting your community's amenity package and the sales center, or providing an overview of the entire construction process, narrated by the company president, is best left to the professional videographer. If you pay for professional video, also get the copyright for it so you

Study Your Competition

1. Go online to your top three competitors' sites.
2. Browse the sites, noting their advanced functionality, if any.
3. Go to your favorite three sites outside the home building industry.
4. Browse them and note their advanced functionality.
5. Keep your list of sites and notes to use later in this chapter.

can have unlimited use of the video on your website, Facebook page, blog, YouTube channel, and all other social media sites. Also get the video in a format your web developer can work with. I like MPEG-4 best, but FLV, WMV, and MOV also work. Ask your web developer which they prefer.

- **Games and animation.** Be creative! Devise games or otherwise use animation to enhance or replace static content on your website. For example, you could use mouse-over display effects on a construction timeline or feature your company's history in a slide show. However, as discussed previously, flash features like these should be limited to a component on a page, rather than taking an entire page. You will need to perform a few extra SEO steps to allow the search engines to read and index some files. Chapter 3 will discuss SEO in more detail.

When your site is fun, interactive, entertaining, and provides quick access to information, visitors will want to return. Use your website to demonstrate pride in your company and in its products, and to show how happy your customers are that they chose to buy one of your homes.

Effectiveness

After creating a website designed to attract buyers with the right content and a high "coolness" factor, you must ensure it works. As discussed previously, the primary goal for your website should be to generate so much

Show Your Affinity

As a member of NAHB, you can add the organization's logo to your website with a link to http://www.nahb.org. If you are a home builder, this can enhance your credibility and demonstrate to potential home buyers that you are a professional builder. If you supply products to the home building industry, having the NAHB logo on your site shows your affinity with the federation, which promotes members doing business with members.

excitement that home buyers are compelled to visit your sales center or contact your sales staff. With the vast majority of home buyers using the Internet to look for homes, the job of your website and your team is to get these buyers from the Internet to your sales center. Chapter 6 will discuss converting web leads into sales center visitors and chapter 7 will discuss in detail all of the KPIs to consider in your overall marketing program. For now, let me explain how to measure your website's effectiveness by analyzing the traffic it attracts, requests for contact, and the number of visitors who contact you after visiting your website.

Call to Action

A call to action is a link or a statement on your website that encourages website visitors to do something before leaving your site, instead of just browsing. The most basic and obvious calls to action include putting your sales office phone number and instructions to call on each page of your website and adding a "contact us" link on the top right side of your site. That link should open an e-mail form that collects a prospect's information and sends it to your sales team. Provide your visitors—including leads, prospects, buyers under contract, and existing home owners—with specific instructions for contacting you. You cannot assume they will think to contact you without being prompted or spend time to seek out a form or your phone number. Other effective calls to action include the following:

- Schedule an appointment.
- Schedule a private home tour.
- Contact us.
- Chat online.
- Subscribe to our newsletter.
- Subscribe to our *RSS feed*.
- Click for VIP promotions.
- Watch our videos.

Having an effective call to action on every page creates an atmosphere of trust and a sense of community. Encouraging prospects to interact with you will keep you on their short list of home builders, will help build your credibility, and will eventually lead to home purchases.

Scaling Up

As you build your online presence and begin to attract more qualified leads, your website must be able to grow with your company. You must plan for advanced capabilities in the future that will not add significant overhead or require you to rebuild when it is time to scale up your strategy. Ask your web developers these three questions:

1. How will new communities or plans be added to the site?
2. How will the icon be added to the Google Map for a new community?
3. Will the site be able to handle more web traffic than the current amount?

You don't want to outgrow your website; you want to be able to build on it to keep it current, relevant, and effective.

You also want your website to be manageable so your administrative staff without technical expertise can update the content. Your web developer should build an administrative tool or use a *content management system (CMS)* that doesn't require programming skills to update most of the content. Ask your developer to create an individual file, an "include file," which contains code for you to use on multiple pages of your website. This will minimize the need to manually change your website's most common elements (i.e., the top navigation). For example, some websites are created with each page of the website built completely separate from the rest of the website. In this case, if you decided to add a new community or a new page to your website, you would need to go into every page of your website to add a link to that page. Creating a website with a single file that contains common code for use on multiple pages makes it easy to update. All your developer would need to do is update the single file. The new code would then be automatically added to all other pages that file is included on.

It is also important to ensure that your developer is using a common programming language to create your website so you won't have to depend on one individual to manage updates or redesigns. *Ruby on Rails, Drupal,* and *Joomla* are among the CMS systems that require more advanced technical skills to update. As a web developer, I can use any of the CMS systems, and sometimes I even like to manually code websites directly without a CMS. However, my preferred language to develop in is *PHP*, and my preferred CMS is WordPress. WordPress and the other CMS options mentioned are all built on PHP architecture. My clients also like WordPress because it is easy to use and we can customize their site's administration based on the skill of their staffs much easier than with other, more technical, CMS options. Just as remodeling a home requires professional expertise but regular maintenance is the home owner's responsibility, you will always require a professional web developer to manage complex changes to your website. But you shouldn't need to pay a professional each time you want to update your price list. WordPress is an effective CMS, built in PHP, which provides a very easy-to-use administrative tool.

The Mobile Web

All websites I build for clients are mobile enabled. With the growth in web visitors browsing from their smartphones, you should also build mobile capabilities into your website. Of all the traffic we track to our client sites and our internal websites every month, just over 10% of the traffic was visiting from a smartphone or mobile device as of September 2011. This is up from 4%–6% in September 2010.

A potential buyer looking for homes using their phone should find useful information on, and be able to use, your website. This can be tricky because you don't want to sacrifice the desktop or laptop users' experiences in the process. When designing and building your site to be mobile friendly, consider these three options: *mobile enabled, mobile website* and *mobile applications* (mobile apps).

Mobile-enabled Websites

All of the sites we build currently are "mobile enabled." This means they look fine when viewed on a mobile device and visitors will be able to find what they are looking for. Although some features may not be compatible with mobile web browsers and some functionality may be missing when visitors are using mobile devices, visitors on your website still will have a positive experience. Two specific examples of common website features that might not work correctly are some of the Google Map, API, and Flash elements. Also, an image-heavy website, even when the images are optimized for the Internet, will load very slowly on a smartphone because the cellular network connection is substantially slower than the Internet connection you may have at home or office. Most mobile-enabled sites will work fine on mobile devices and will offer the web visitor the content they are looking for, but some have a few minor limitations.

Mobile Websites

Mobile websites are specifically designed to be viewed on a handheld device with a slower connection, lower resolution, and smaller screen size than a computer's. These sites are built for cell phones, iPads, and other mobile devices. They load quickly, are designed for a smaller screen, and contain few or no images. They enable visitors to get the information they are looking for quickly and easily. Your web developer can embed code in your website that will determine when a visitor is using a mobile device and automatically send the person to the site created for mobile viewing.

> ### Quick-Response (QR) Codes and Text Messaging
>
> QR codes are two-dimensional codes, similar to bar codes, which allow smartphones with a QR code reader to scan the code and be directed to a web page, video, or other content. Home builders are placing QR codes on their signage so visitors can get information even when the sales office and model home are closed.
>
> You can also create a mobile text site, which works like this: when a user texts a word to a designated number, they receive an instant and automated text message reply. Instant information, such as a flyer or driving directions, can be delivered to a home buyer's cell phone while they are standing in front of a spec home. One cool feature on a text site is that it captures the home buyer's cell phone number. Text "mrelevance" (without the quotation marks) to 99699 for an example of a mobile text site.

Mobile visitors usually are not looking for a photo gallery; they are looking for facts and information quickly. An electronic data sheet about a particular home or community (like the brochures you leave outside a of home for sale) works well on a mobile website. Include a link to your main website and tell users they can view photos and more information there.

Mobile Applications

Mobile applications, or mobile apps, are downloadable applications that reside and run on the mobile device, rather than relying on the mobile device's web browser. Both free and paid applications are available from iTunes, Android Marketplace, and other online application stores.

Mobile apps cost thousands of dollars or more to build and may have limited relevance for home builders. Most people probably would not download an app to their smart phone just to see your company's inventory, for

Understanding the Difference Between Mobile-Enabled and Mobile Sites

1. Get your smart phone or tablet (iPhone, Android device, iPad, etc.). If you don't have one, you need to upgrade your current phone. You will have difficulty competing without a smart phone.
2. Sit at your computer with the mobile device.
3. Open the web browser on your computer and on the smart phone.
4. Go to http://www.sighomes.com on each device.
5. Note what you see on each site.
6. Go to your website on each device.
7. Note the differences between what you see on each site.

example. They may, however, download an app that has all the listings in the market. Your home buyer might download an app specific to your company that updates the construction progress on their home or allows them to request and follow warranty work. For now, however, new home marketers should master how to use mobile-enabled and mobile websites effectively.

Landing Pages

A landing page is the specific web page where web visitors arrive on your website. Most visitors will land on your home page. The landing page is an important consideration for lead management, prospect identification, and conversion. It is among the most effective, but unfortunately underused, marketing techniques. Creating landing pages is an easy strategy for attracting warm prospects to your website and identifying them when they visit. When you need to provide a specific link for a unique audience, like local newspaper readers or Facebook users, you can customize a landing page for them so they have the right frame of reference when they get to your website.

For example, if you are running a banner ad on your local newspaper site for an incentive in one of your communities, you can build a unique landing page for that specific marketing campaign. When the web visitor clicks the link, you know they are interested in the incentive. The landing page instantly transforms a cold lead into a warm one.

You can increase your landing page's effectiveness in generating leads by offering incentives for visitors to answer an additional call to action. For example, ask them to "Enter the following information" to

- hear about promotions early;
- win a $10 gas card; or
- get a free upgrade package.

Make sure your form is simple. Ask for only three to four fields of information. The GVG Homes landing page is simple, fresh, and eye-catching (fig. 2.13). It is also contained within the website's framework so web visitors land on the page, fill out the short form, and can then continue to navigate through the rest of the site. Be careful not to trap warm leads on a cool page with nowhere else to go.

Budgeting

Consider three factors when developing budgets for your website development or redesign:

1. Initial capital outlay
2. Ongoing maintenance
3. Internal resources, including available staff and their skill level

As you develop your plan to build a website from scratch or redesign your existing site, bear in mind that your website is an ongoing project

GVG Homes Landing Page

This clean landing page includes a concise data entry form. (Reprinted with permission from Greater Valley Group, West Point, Georgia)

Sample Budget for a Builder of 25 Homes per Year

For a builder who builds 25 homes per year with an average sale price of $500,000, the calculation for determining an Internet marketing budget is as follows:

25 homes/yr × $500,000 (average sales price)
= $12,500,000 (top-line revenue)

$12,500,000 × 1.5% = $187,500 (total annual marketing budget)

$187,500 × 50% = $93,750 (fixed marketing costs)

$93,750 × 70% = $65,625 (annual Internet marketing budget)

with many layers. Because it is the essential tool for Internet marketing, you will have to continually update it with timely, relevant information.

The cost to build your new site will depend on your needs and company requirements. I have built hundreds of sites, some for as little as $1,500 with little functionality and some that cost more than $500,000 with complex databases, CRM applications, and back-office integration. The following guidelines will help you determine how much your company should spend.

The National Sales and Marketing Council estimates a builder's total marketing budget (including all marketing, not just Internet marketing) should be roughly 1%–1.5% of top-line revenue, with smaller companies at the high end or slightly above that range. *Fixed marketing costs* such as model merchandising, product research, brochures, and other expenses not tied directly to promotion, communication, and marketing make up about half of that total budget. Sixty to seventy percent of the remainder for *variable marketing costs* should be spent on Internet marketing, including development, setup, upgrades, updates, and adding functionality. The remaining budget should be spent on traditional advertising and signage. Using these guidelines, you should be able to estimate your marketing and Internet marketing budget.

A large national builder might budget $100,000–$250,000 or more for an initial web development project with custom integration, whereas a custom builder, small-volume builder, or remodeler might budget $5,000–$35,000. We build many websites in the $12,000–$20,000 range with sufficient functionality. If you are similar to the builder in the example with a budget of roughly $65,000 per year and you spend $20,000 on your website, you have about $4,000 a month left to promote the website online and $28,000 for traditional advertising and other content creation. No matter which category your company is in, you must have an operating budget for updating, enhancing, and adding functionality to your website. Technology and business changes that have occurred recently require that your website be rebuilt, redesigned, or refreshed about every three years. New technology continually emerges and you want to remain on the leading edge in adopting new tools to maintain your online competitive advantage.

Next Steps

Now that you understand the power of a website in new home marketing and sales, essential features to include, and some measures of its effectiveness, you are ready to start building or redesigning your website. Follow these steps:

- Review the notes you took from the four exercises from the chapter.
  - Website Goal Setting
  - Competitor Shop for Functionality
  - Scavenger Hunt Usability
  - Mobile Site vs. Mobile Enabled
- Review your website, asking the following key questions about the five essential website elements discussed in this chapter.
  1. Rich and Relevant Content
     - Are my buyers finding all the information about my homes online?
     - Is the content well written, free of typos and other mistakes, and keyword rich?
     - Is it relevant to the search engines and web visitors?
     - Does it allow buyers to find the information they want to know?
  2. Intuitive Navigation
     - Are top-level navigation links limited to seven or fewer?
     - Is it easy for visitors to find any information in less than two or three clicks, from several different starting points?
     - Does my website pass the scavenger hunt test?
  3. Attractive Design
     - Is the website pleasing to the eye?
     - Am I proud to send people there?
     - Does it build my brand and credibility throughout the site?

4. Functionality–the "Coolness" factor
   - Is my site interactive?
   - Does it give visitors a reason to return?
   - Does it demonstrate advanced technology?
5. Effectiveness
   - Is there an effective call to action on every page of the website?
   - Is there an address, phone number, or other contact information on each page of the website?
   - Am I sending all traffic to the main home page or do I use landing pages as appropriate?
   - Is the site generating leads and prospects?

■ Refine your goals for your website. List and prioritize the functionality you want to add (must have, nice to have, would like but not necessary) so you can draft a budget. Then, talk to a few experienced web developers about your list. You can find them through your local HBA or NAHB. Ask for their recommendations and for a cost estimate for redesigning and reprogramming your website, and adding to it in the future.

Search Engine Optimization 3

Once you have a brilliantly designed website, you need SEO. The goal of SEO is to have your website appear on the first page of Google results and the other search engines when a user types in your targeted keywords. You want Google to list your website first when home buyers search, and you want to fill up all or as much of the page as possible with links to positive content about your company, including links to your websites and blogs. If you can fill up Google with positive content about your company for several keyword searches, the traffic and buyers will find you. You will need more than just a website to do this because each site can have only two links on the search engine results page. Your blog, other sites where you can publish content and social media sites can help you improve your SERPs by giving you more chances for your positive content to be listed on the first page of the search engines.

Think about it this way: building an effective SEO program is like putting a billboard (your website) on several prominent highways (search engines). More than 80% of online searches start on Google. Target the right keywords on Google and you will drive quality traffic to your website.

Using Google as an example, here's how search engines work: When you type words into the search box on a search engine, the search results page returned is divided into two sections. The top shaded section and right sidebar "sponsored links" are paid advertisements. The sites that appear there pay the search engine for every visitor that clicks on that link. The center of the page is where *organic search results* appear. These are not paid advertisements. They appear in the list in a given order according to their relevance as deemed by the search engine bots. The higher a website or link is in the SERPs, the more relevant it is to the search term. Consumers are more likely to click the top organic results than the sponsored links. In fact, the top three organic search engine placements are viewed 100% of the time, whereas the top three sponsored locations are viewed, respectively, only 50%, 40%, and 30% of the time.[3]

Google's organic SERP listings appear in order of their relevance to the searched keyword(s). For example, if you Google "Mitch Levinson," the first page shows the top 10 results most relevant for my name. Getting your sites and content listed on the first page of your SERPs for your targeted keywords is one goal of SEO. Consumers view the top-ranked organic sites listed on the first page as the premier authorities for their search. Try to fill up that page, and subsequent pages if possible, with your content.

As previously mentioned, Google has several software programs (bots and spiders) designed to crawl the web and index every page online. These bots go from page to page, reading the content, identifying relevant keywords and visiting every link. They index every page of relevant content and associate the page to relevant words. This is how Google determines the list of results for each search term.

Page Rank and Other Variables

None of the search engines reveals the variables used in their algorithms, mathematical formulas which determine the order that the results page lists the sites. The algorithms change frequently (Google adjusted its algorithm more than 400 times in 2010). After working in Internet marketing for more than a decade, I can only guess at the variables used to rank search results. Anyone who says they know exactly what is in the algorithm is either lying or is named Larry Page or Sergey Brin (the founders of Google).

PageRank (PR), named for Larry Page, the creator of the original algorithm, is a score Google attributes to each website indexed. A page can rank from 0 to 10. Google has a PR of 10. At the time this book was written, Amazon's and eBay's scores were, respectively, 9 and 8. Most home builder website PR scores range from 2 to 5. The rank was first based on the website's popularity, among other variables. Although popularity probably is still a factor, it may only be one of the variables in the algorithm that determines search results.

Other factors, such as traffic and longevity, may also be part of the algorithm variables. For instance, some search engine experts believe the longer people stay on your site, or the stickier it is, the higher your PR score will be. Some experts also say the older your site is and the longer you have the *domain name* reserved, the higher your PR score will be. A site that was originally launched in 2002 (even if it has been redesigned several times since it was created) and is not up for renewal until 2020 would score better on this metric than a site launched last year on a domain name purchased for one year only. The important thing for you to remember, though, is that SEO techniques will help improve your PR score and relevant rankings no matter when your site launched, so give the search engines the food they need.

By using the right SEO techniques, you can get the search engine bots to: 1) visit your site quickly, 2) return to your site more often, and 3) index your site and its content for the relevant words you are targeting. If Google visits your site often and ranks it as relevant for your targeted keywords, your site will appear higher in SERPs than other sites visited less often that do not have a relevant keyword strategy. Search engines read website content to determine its relevance to a given search term or topic. The more relevant the site is to word phrases, the higher that site appears on a SERP and the more searches the site appears in. The more often your website appears on a SERP, the more traffic you will get.

Using Keywords

Developing an effective keyword strategy is part science and part art. To get maximum *search volume,* target web searchers who do not know you or the name of your company. Ask yourself what words prospects will type into the search box when they get to Google. You want to capture anyone online who might be interested in your product. Choose keywords that

- have enough search volume (appear most often) in searches for what you are selling;
- are relevant to your company, your industry, or your product in the minds of buyers who are not familiar with your company; and
- seem realistic in terms of how competitive the keyword is and how likely it is for you to elevate your search results relative to your competition.

A Formula for Success

The first thing I do when creating a keyword strategy is to brainstorm with my clients about the types of words to use. We compile word phrases in a list. For instance, my home builder clients generally start with location descriptors (city, county, or whatever makes sense locally), broad product category descriptors (homes, condos, townhomes), and narrower product type descriptors (new homes, real estate, green building).

Second, I view *Google Analytics* or whatever website tracking software is on the website I am optimizing to see which search terms are already driving traffic to the site.

Third, I visit my competitor sites and look at their words.

Finally, I go to Google and begin searching words, noting the suggestions Google offers automatically while I type. Because Google provides these suggested terms, you can deduce that they are popular searches so you should probably adopt them for your SEO. Obviously these terms are most popular and most used or Google would not recommend them.

Once I have a comprehensive list of words in each category, sometimes as many as 10 or 12 for each, I go to Google Trends (http://www.google.com/trends) and Google *Adword's* Keyword tool (http://www.google.com/adwords) to search each word phrase individually. Neither site shows you how many times a particular word is searched, but you can see a term's relative ranking compared with other terms within the same general category. For example, Google Trends recently weighted real estate 1.00, homes 0.88, and builders 0.14. Similarly, Google applied a weight of 1.00 to Bay Area, 0.36 to Roseville, and 2.20 to Sacramento. I develop various combinations of words and apply math to rank the most effective words in a list for my SEO campaign.

I then create a matrix of these word phrases, combined effectively, with their new weight (i.e., the term Sacramento homes has the weight of $2.20 \times 0.88 = 1.94$). Typically I put the location word first because generally it attracts more search volume that way. Creating keyword phrases is a manual process that occasionally needs to be tweaked from a marketing standpoint. In other words, the content of Table 3.1 is refined into Table 3.2.

Once I have the combined and weighted list, I go to Google and search each word to see how many sites are already ranked for that word. At the top of the Google search page is the number of results for that word. This is the number

TABLE 3.1   Weighted Keywords

Bay Area	1	real estate	1
Bay Area	1	homes	0.88
Bay Area	1	builders	0.14
Roseville	0.36	real estate	1
Roseville	0.36	homes	0.88
Roseville	0.36	builders	0.14
Sacramento	2.2	real estate	1
Sacramento	2.2	homes	0.88
Sacramento	2.2	builders	0.14

of competing sites for the word. I use these numbers to again apply math to score and rank my list of words. The higher the score, the better the word. That was all science. Creating the actual list of keywords I will target, though, is an art. Table 3.3 shows a sample list of keywords for this example.

TABLE 3.2	Weighted Keyword Phrases
Bay Area real estate	1
Bay Area homes	0.88
Bay Area builders	0.14
Roseville real estate	0.36
Roseville homes	0.3168
Roseville builders	0.0504
Sacramento real estate	2.2
Sacramento homes	1.936
Sacramento builders	0.308

If this list were created for a small custom home builder, I would not recommend that they optimize for the term "Sacramento real estate." It is a commonly used and highly competitive term so trying to get a site to rank high for it would be labor intensive and costly. It would be very difficult to get a small custom builder on the first page of Google using that term. "Sacramento builders," "Roseville real estate," and "Bay area builders" are much more realistic and likely to deliver better results to a small custom builder's SEO campaign. That is the art–selecting the right keywords that realistically can get your site on page one of search engine results and actually drive traffic to your website.

Keep in mind that a list of nine keyword phrases is a fraction of possible word combinations you could optimize your website for. When we brainstorm with clients, the initial list can grow to more than 100 words. But you can't effectively optimize a single website for 100 words immediately, so start with 5–15 words.

Keep your complete list, though, and prioritize 15 secondary and 15 tertiary words in addition to your top choices. Use this list of 35–45 keywords to establish a benchmark for your SEO campaign by typing each term into a search engine and noting where your website appears (if at all) in the results. Make sure you are logged out of the search engines so their algorithms do not factor your web browsing history into the equation. (Search engines capture your web browsing history so

TABLE 3.3 Keyword Phrases

Word Phrase	Weight	Competition	Score
Sacramento real estate	2.2	37,900,000	83,380,000
Sacramento homes	1.936	31,100,000	60,209,600
Bay Area real estate	1	42,900,000	42,900,000
Bay Area homes	0.88	38,500,000	33,880,000
Sacramento builders	0.308	7,040,000	2,168,320
Roseville real estate	0.36	5,630,000	2,026,800
Roseville homes	0.3168	3,950,000	1,251,360
Bay Area builders	0.14	7,010,000	981,400
Roseville builders	0.0504	2,280,000	114,912

Selecting Keywords

1. Don't be too aggressive. Start with a few words and add to your list periodically.
2. Be realistic in your word choice. Don't try to compete for keywords against companies with deep pockets.
3. Monitor and evaluate the results of your SEO campaign over time. Moving up in the search engines is a gradual process.

if you visit your website more than other websites, it may rank artificially high when you are logged in compared with a typical user's search results.)

I also use RankChecker by SEO-Book to view my search engine rankings (fig. 3.1). This application works with *Firefox,* a web browser like Internet Explorer, Chrome, and Safari. Go to http://tools.seobook.com/firefox/rank-checker/ to download the free *plug-in.* It will install a toolbar on your browser window with an icon you click to run the RankChecker application. Type in the website address you want to find and the keywords you want to check, click Start, and RankChecker does the rest. The application is not perfect, but you will have a benchmark for your current ranking in the search engines and an indicator of how you need to adjust your prioritized list of words.

Keyword Selection Exercise

The following exercise will help you select and begin to target the best words for your company:

1. Create your list of words, including location, product type, and industry words.
2. Go to Google Trends and find the traffic value for each word.
3. Compile the list of words with their trend values.
4. Pair each location word with each of the other words.

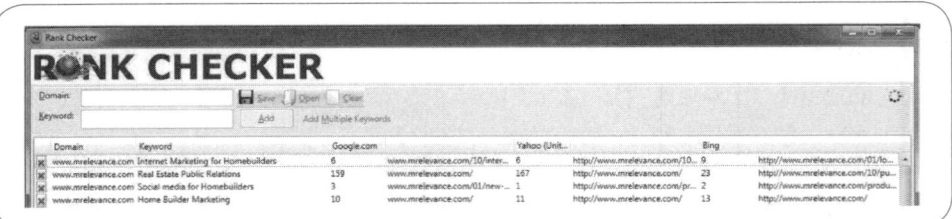

 RankChecker

RankChecker shows where a website ranks in search engine results for a specific keyword. (Reprinted with permission from SEOBook)

5. Multiply the trend values of the location word and the word it's paired with.
6. Reorder the full list of words and trend values based on the adjusted value of the combined words (location × other words).
7. Google each word phrase on the list and note how many sites are indexed for that word phrase.
8. Multiply the adjusted trend value by the competition to arrive at a score. (For example, if the adjusted trend value is 3.2 and the number of competitive sites is 1.2 million, the score would be calculated as follows: 3.2 × 1,200,000 = 3,840,000.)
9. Sort by score, highest to lowest.
10. Review the list and slightly rearrange the words as appropriate, considering marketing and your locality.
11. Prioritize the list in terms of primary, secondary, and tertiary words.
12. Run RankChecker on the top words in the new list

How did your site rank for each of your new targeted word phrases? Keep this list and re-run the RankChecker report on a regular basis to monitor how your site moves in the rankings for your targeted primary words.

Google SEO Tools

There are SEO tools in addition to RankChecker, which are listed in the Resources at the back of the book. One that is a must for every site is Google Webmaster Tools (WMT). I use it regularly and on every site I launch because it is one of the most useful places to see SEO issues with your site. You submit a *site map* to WMT and the program reveals errors, such as broken links and other crawler issues, on your site. It also shows the keywords it finds and ranks your site for, reviews your *robots.txt file,* and even suggests ways to improve the ranking for your site in the search engines. To find WMT, log into your Google account and type webmaster tools in the search box or go to http://www.google.com/webmasters/tools while logged into your account.

A site map, in this context, is a file of all the pages on your website with links to those pages. Basically, it is a high-level outline of every page on your site. Different from site maps for consumers that are an index of the pages on a website, these site maps are designed specifically for the search engines to have an easy reference to crawl and index all of the pages on your website. Typically, the search engines like site maps

SEO Essentials

- Use both on- and off-page SEO techniques to boost your website's ranking on SERPs for your targeted keywords.
- Enter *title tags* and H tags for maximum impact and write effective anchor text.
- Construct internal and inbound links strategically, striving to earn links to your pages from other relevant websites.

in XML format, which is an Internet language for transferring and displaying data. But the format is not as important as the site map itself. Google has a tool, found in WMT, that will create an XML site map for you, or you can go to Google and search for "XML site map generators" and pick one. You will have to run the site map's software and add a file to your website, but it will be well worth it.

Robots.txt files are just as important. These files tell the search engines what to crawl and index, and what to ignore. For example, if your website has an administrative tool on the back end, you probably don't want the search engines to crawl those pages. If you have a database, private folders, or even online assets and some photo galleries, you may want to reference them in the Robots.txt file. Again, this is a simple file that just needs to be added to your website's main directory. Most Robots.txt files contain the following content:

```
User-agent: *
Disallow:
Sitemap: http://www.mitchlevinson.com/site map.xml.gz
```

This tells all search engines (User-Agent: *) what pages on the site not to follow. The example below tells the search engines not to index the folder called admin:

```
User-Agent: *
Disallow: /admin/
Sitemap: http://www.mitchlevinson.com/site map.xml.gz
```

Robots.txt files are a relatively simple way to give the search engines a file to make their indexing more efficient.

SEO Techniques

SEO strategies fall into one of two categories, on-page or off-page. As the names imply, *on-page SEO* refers to the changes made and techniques used directly on the pages of your website. Conversely, *off-page SEO* comprises techniques you can use elsewhere online. On-page

SEO establishes your website's relevance and credibility. Off-page SEO positions you as an industry authority as other websites link to yours.

On-Page SEO

On-page SEO tells the search engines what your site is about, gives the search engines the relevant words that you want to be indexed for, and feeds them new content frequently enough so they return to your site regularly. If you do these three things effectively, you will elevate your website on the search engine results pages and drive natural search traffic to your website. Consider the keywords identified in the last exercise as the food you need to feed the search engine bots. Those keywords are essential to accomplishing these objectives. You must integrate them into your company vocabulary, marketing collateral, and other written material. I have been accused of thinking more like a search engine than a home buyer at times, and I think that is good. Whenever I consider my Internet marketing strategy, especially search engine optimization, I think about how I will use my keywords.

Title Tags

Title tags are the first, and possibly the most important, on-page SEO element. Every web page has a title,

Avoid Black-Hat Trickery

It is no secret that the search engines do not like SEO companies; they think that we try to "manipulate" their search results for the SEO client's gain. Of course, that is exactly what we are trying to do: display our websites high in the results pages for our relevant words. All the techniques this book recommends are *white-hat SEO*—generally accepted and proven effective over time. These techniques don't artificially manipulate the search engines as much as they represent to the search engines the strength of the actual content of the website. Some other SEO companies employ techniques that are considered *black-hat SEO*. These are designed to trick the search engines to think the website is more relevant for a word than it really is. Although black-hat techniques may drive some traffic in the short term, when Google or any other search engine determines you are using them, they will remove your website from their index completely. Black-hat techniques falsely represent the relevance of a website to the search engines and trick users into viewing pages that don't have the content they were looking for.

Tag spamming or *keyword spamming* is one black-hat technique. This technique repeats your keywords on your site a significant number of times to artificially produce a higher percentage of keywords relative to the total number of words and content on the site, otherwise called *keyword density*. These additional and repeated keywords may be in the original content or completely divorced from page content, and the spamming may be visible or invisible to visitors. For example, I could type the words "new homes in Raleigh" 100 times at the bottom of my site to try to fool the search engines. This is not the same thing as writing keyword-rich content that accurately represents your company and products, and which makes sense to readers. Trying to fool the search engines can get your site removed from Google search result pages permanently.

FIGURE 3.2 mRELEVANCE Title Tag
The website title uses specific and effective keywords in the title tag to describe page content to the search engines. (Reprinted with permission from mRELEVANCE LLC)

which appears at the top of the browser, within the browser window (fig. 3.2).

The mRELEVANCE home page title is "mRELEVANCE | Websites, Social Media, Search Engine Optimization and Public Relations | Home Builder Marketing." This title tag is the first thing the Googlebot sees when visiting the site, so it is the single most important and effective on-page SEO technique. It should tell the search engines exactly what the site is about. I can't count the number of times I visit a site where the title is simply the name of the company or "home page." What words do those titles tell Google to index your site and web pages for?

Not only is the page title the first thing Google reads, it also appears on the SERP as the actual link to your website. Therefore, it is the most important phrase you will write. Each page should have a unique title relevant to its content that includes your targeted keywords. Having multiple pages indexed with the title "Welcome to Levinson Builders" does not tell the search engines (or consumers for that matter) what your site or each page is about. You must take the time to develop a list of targeted keywords and use those words to carefully craft the titles of each and every page on your website, especially the most important pages. These are most likely the ones in your top-level navigation, and possibly even your second-tier pages.

After you have written them, adding title tags to your pages is easy. Just type them between an opening tag (<title>) and a closing tag (</title>) at the top of your webpage somewhere between the <head> and </head> tags (fig. 3.3). If you are using a CMS, there is probably a field where you can add a title. You will see the title shown displays when you go to my website.

Keywords and URLs

The URL or domain name for your website is also an opportunity to highlight keywords, although this strategy is not as easy as writing keyword-rich titles. Use keywords in your domain name when you can, but because your domain name typically reflects your brand or company name, don't worry too much if you can't incorporate keywords there. You can also purchase and redirect additional keyword-rich domain names to your website, but be sure to send links and traffic to your website through those domain names. For example, the HBA of Greater Austin has purchased the domain name, www.austinhomebuilders.com. Therefore, when a user types that text in a browser they are redirected to www.hbaaustin.com.

Keyword and Description Tags

In addition to the title tags at the top of web pages, the search engines also read other *metadata,* information embedded in a website's coding, that describes that website. SEO experts disagree about whether these tags can boost your search ranking. Although I agree that some of the search engines do not use much metadata, I recommend tagging pages to ensure the search engines represent your web pages accurately.

An item in a Google SERP list shows not only the page title, but also a brief description of the page. That description must encourage

```
<div class="entry clearfix">
    <a href="http://www.atlantarealestateforum.com/grand-vacation-destination-now-offers-
atlanta-new-homes-40666/" rel="bookmark" title="Permanent Link to Grand Vacation Destination
Now Offers Atlanta New Homes"><img src="http://www.atlantarealestateforum.com/wp-content/
photos/2010/11/abnhtv.png" class="post-thum" alt="post thumbnail" /></a>
    <h2><a href="http://www.atlantarealestateforum.com/grand-vacation-destination-now-offers-
atlanta-new-homes-40666/" rel="bookmark title="Permanent Link to Grand Vacation Destination Now
Offers Atlanta New Homes">Grand Vacation Destination Now Offers Atlanta New Homes</a></h2>
    <p>Callaway Gardens is known throughout the Southeast as a premier vacation destination, and
now it offers residential homes to its blend of nature and golf thanks to Cousins Properties.
The builder has been developing the Atlanta real estate in Callaway Gardens for the past four
to five years and offes a variety of home styles [...]</p>
```

FIGURE 3.3 mRELEVANCE Metadata
Web page data coded in *hypertext markup language (HTML,*. (Reprinted with permission from mRELEVANCE LLC)

web visitors to go to your site instead of to other companies' listed on the same SERP. If you have not included a meta-description for your page in the code, Google will create its own. Without an actual description tag, Google uses the first words and content on the page as the description. These might actually be the headings in your navigation bar. In that case, your description will be a list of words that will confuse home buyers, rather than encourage them to pick you over your results-page competitors. Creating your own descriptions instead of relying on the search engines to automatically generate them is another way to control the information Internet users see about your company.

The keyword metadata tag encompasses keywords you want the search engines to index your site for. It can be a laundry list of all the words for which you want to be indexed. Although Google officially states that its search engine does not use keyword metadata to index websites, other search engines may use it. You don't need to add keyword metadata to all your pages, but you should add it to the specific and targeted pages you want the search engines to index first: pages with information on your company and homes and with the most effective calls to action. Keyword metadata must incorporate keywords consistent with the title tag on the web page.

Content

Search engines also read the content on each page to index your site in the SERPs for relevant words. Keep the text focused and concise (75–250 words per page) and effectively use the appropriate keywords. Keyword density is the number of times you use a particular keyword on a given page as a percentage of total words on that page. For instance, if you write 100 words on a page and your keyword "homes" is used 3 times on that page, the keyword density of that word is 3%. Density of more than 5% may be considered keyword spamming, so strive for a density of 1% to 5%.

Editing with Keywords

Writing effective keyword-rich text is not as easy as it may seem. It takes time and thought. To write keyword-rich content, first write your text. Make it informational, readable, and lively. Then go back and edit the text to add keywords where appropriate. Make sure to use the appropriate number of keywords so the search engines understand the relevance of the topic, and readers still find it interesting.

Tag Hierarchy

You can also code specific text elements with tags to indicate their importance. Search engines consider tag hierarchy to evaluate a text's relevance for specific words. Tag hierarchy begins at the highest level with H1 tags and extends through H6. A web page title is an H1 tag, the first subheading or highlighted words within a paragraph might be an H2 tag, and so on. On the mRELEVANCE web page shown in fig. 3.2, the H2 tag could be used for the boldface words in the introductory paragraph ("the intersection of social and search" and "traditional PR, social media, and search engine optimization"). The H3 tag could be used to indicate the significance of the words "Marketing Relevance," "Teaching Relevance," and "Products and Services."

Just like the other tags discussed, the h tags are easy to add. Use both an opening and closing tag like this: <h3>Products and Services</h>

Additional Tags

There are also tags that correspond to images and links. *Link titles* appear when a visitor hovers his or her mouse pointer over a word or words in hyperlinked text. *ALT tags* appear when the visitor hovers the mouse pointer over an image. Figure 3.3 illustrates that the code for the images that includes the ALT tag is <img src=http://www.atlantarealestateforum.com/wp-content/photos/2010/11/abnhtv.jpg class="post-thum" alt="post thumbnail"/> and the title for both the link and the image is "Permanent Link to Grand Vacation Destination Now Offers Atlanta New Homes."

Just as you would add metadata to web page code, when you upload an image or create a link to a website, you need to add the appropriate tags. Search engines cannot read images so they can't assess their relevance without ALT tags and a keyword-rich image name. Make sure to use these tags, and also try to use keywords in the file names of the images.

Off-Page SEO

Off-page SEO techniques are used on a website other than your own. They include links and words—the clickable text and the links back to your site from another website.

Anchor Text

Anchor text is the clickable text on a web page—the text with a *hyperlink* attached to it. It tells the search engine about the topic of the page the link will open. Keyword-rich anchor text on an external website that links to your web page with a keyword-rich title reinforces the site's relevance. The text "Click here for information about new homes in Raleigh" is not effective, but "Want more information about new homes in Raleigh?" is. Always use effective anchor text to secure links from other websites.

Budget

Like every other aspect of effective marketing, SEO requires time and money. You must conduct research, select the right keywords, implement on-page and off-page strategies, and monitor results weekly and over time. Many companies offer SEO services; many also will try to sell you "vaporware," a bill of goods without accountability for results. You can spend as little as $500 per month or more than $2,000 on SEO. Rebuilding a website to be search-engine friendly is sometimes more cost effective than trying to incorporate SEO into an existing website. Spend your money wisely and work with the right companies to get the best results. Selecting the right company is easy. Ask vendors what sites they have optimized and for what words. Then go to Google and find out for yourself how they did.

Using targeted keywords as anchor text tells the search engine what the page is going to is about. It demonstrates the relevance of the words to the page and gives the search engines context to index the linked page.

Link Building

Like your keyword strategy, the recipe for building links to and from your site is part science and part art. You want other relevant sites to link to yours and you want to link to other sites that provide content valuable to your audience. Websites with a higher PR score are more relevant so they are good places to get links from. Linking to or having links from sites the search engines score low for relevance can lower your ranking on the SERP. As a rule, my company structures outbound links to open in a new browser window even if we are linking to a site that provides valuable content. You can also add a *no-follow tag* to links. This tag prevents the site to which you are referring from improving its relevance because of your link. Sometimes the search engines interpret this tag as an advertising link, however, so use it sparingly to maintain your site's relevance in the search engines. Sites that allow advertising generally do not rank as high as those that provide non-advertorial content. If a site provides content valuable enough for me to want to link to it, I feel like it has earned whatever increased visibility it gets from me. A good rule of thumb is to only link to pages you find interesting and informative and that you don't mind giving a little boost to in the search engines.

Getting other sites to link to you is more challenging. *Webmasters* compete with your site and others for top rankings in the search engines. Although many factors that influence a web page ranking are unknown, the higher the ranking, the more credibility the web page has, the more value, or *link juice,* the link on a site will send to you. Juice correlates with PR score. Getting links with well-written anchor text from high-scoring sites that don't use no-follow tags can increase your PR score and improve your SERP ranking.

Blogging, Social Media, and Public Relations Strategy

When I ask audiences in my seminars what they think of first when they hear the terms "Internet marketing" and "social media," they almost all say "Facebook." Although Facebook may be a component of social media marketing, social media is much broader than that. Using the Internet to engage, interact, and communicate with your prospects, buyers, or people you want in your network is the crux of social media.

Social media marketing includes creating online profiles, accounts, and web pages that enable communication and conversations within an online sphere of influence. This sphere of influence starts in your network and quickly extends to the entire online community. Your social media program must offer people in your sphere of influence several locations and options to engage with you and your company. Creating an atmosphere for ongoing interaction online helps to build your company's credibility.

Prospective home buyers no longer call your sales office first; instead they text, find you on Facebook, and *tweet* to get more information about your community before they decide whether to contact you. Consumers preparing to make the most significant purchase of their lifetime conduct their preliminary research online. They use social media to find out what they need to know about you and your communities from their sphere of influence, or your sphere of influence, with a click of their mouse or a tap on their smartphone. To gain a competitive edge, put everything they need to know about your company at their fingertips.

In addition, you must control the information that is circulating online about your company's brand and product because information people find about you on the Internet either enhances or detracts from your reputation. It is never neutral. Taking time to publish, distribute, and syndicate content about your company and address questions or comments by others will enhance your company's credibility. Proactively promoting your online brand and message, participating in online discussion about your company, and engaging your prospects and clients openly and transparently—even in negative situations—will contribute to a positive reputation online and in real life.

Customers will talk about you online, whether you want them to or not. Therefore, you must be online where they are, willing to interact with and be scrutinized by them to build your online brand and reputation. Consumers will decide whether or not to pursue a relationship with your company based on what your past customers are saying, how you interact with them, and how you deal with situations in an open forum. You should proactively respond to questions and address touchy situations as they surface. You can influence consumer sentiment and control criticism if you engage online before a complaint explodes, rather than defending your company after the fact. Social media marketing helps you proactively manage buyers' expectations.

Social Media and Online Conversations

Social media allows you to create online conversations that engage others; that is your goal. Whether these conversations occur on a website or blog, on a social networking site or a local search site, you still are responsible for your brand's credibility and your message. These conversations and interactions will happen whether you are engaged or not. In other words, if you decide not to create a social media program because you are afraid people will say negative things about your company, chances are they have already created negative content about you and are currently influencing your online brand and credibility. You need to control your brand before others do it for you. Almost anyone can comment or review any company online, but when you create a thorough social media program and integrate it with your overall Internet marketing strategy, you remain in control of your message.

Social Media Marketing Toolbox

Although creating a company page on Facebook and a corporate account on Twitter are typically considered the minimum requirements for a social media program, social media marketing is much more than simply having your profile on a few social networking sites and attempting to broadcast your message. Take adequate time to research the tools and resources available, how much time you need to create each account, the audience you can reach, and how it will connect to your overall program. This will help you create a program in which various tools interact with and augment one another.

Consider using these resources:

- A company blog
- Microblogs, such as Twitter
- Social networks like Facebook
- Local search, as on Google
- Online public relations (PR)
- Video-sharing sites like You-Tube
- Photo-sharing sites like Picasa and Flickr
- Social bookmarking sites like Digg and Delicious

Social Media Optimization

As with content on your website, you must optimize the content and profiles on social media sites so search engines and consumers can find it easily. *Social media optimization (SMO)* uses social media sites effectively to boost your visibility with the search engines and your communication with your friends, fans, followers, and contacts within your social networks. Follow the same strategies that generally apply to SEO when writing content for your social media pages, blog posts, and online profiles. Use targeted keywords that will saturate Google and other search engines with as much positive information as possible about your company.

Your Own Blog

Google and the other search engines are hungry for fresh food. New keyword-rich content is like a big juicy fly to the search engine spiders. Blogging effectively feeds the search engines regularly and encourages them to return often. When you create a blog, regularly update it, and post on other blogs, you help your social media program satisfy the search engines' appetite for new content. Just as your website forms the foundation of your Internet marketing program, a blog effectively supports your social media program. Therefore, creating and maintaining a blog is your first step and the top priority for your social media marketing program, even before Facebook, Twitter, or other sites in your toolbox.

"What is a blog?" and "How does it differ from a website?" are two common questions people ask. They really aren't much different in that a blog is a type of website. However, they are unlike a traditional website in that each blog post creates a new indexed web page. When you update your website, typically you only replace the content of existing pages so the page count of your website generally remains the same. But on a blog, each new post creates fresh content for the search engines to index. If you post on your blog twice a week, or eight times a month, after a year you will have about 100 new pages of content indexed for your keywords. That is a lot of spider bait! You can see how a blog increases your web presence exponentially. Blogs are an excellent SEO tool because, unlike a traditional website, each new post provides fresh content to entice prospects, buyers, and the search engines.

In addition, the platforms on which blogs are built enable users to add new content easily. Blog posts are dated and display in reverse chronological order (newest entries on top). They started as online journals or diaries where people would write about their day or update their schedules. They were originally called "web logs." Because they facilitate posting fresh content regularly, blogs are a preferred platform for building a company's brand and providing online resources to consumers.

Your blog is a type of website, so when you set it up you still need to consider the five components of a website (content, navigation, design, functionality, and effectiveness). You may apply some of these concepts slightly differently to your blog than you do to your traditional website. Don't be persuaded by companies that offer to build you a free or cheap blog quickly. You don't want to waste time or money on a blog that doesn't improve your SEO for the right keywords. If you don't build your blog properly, it will not enhance your credibility and you will not effectively feed Google.

Rich and Relevant Content

"What should I write about on my blog?" "I'm not sure I have enough happening in my company to write two blog posts a week." If I had a nickel for every time I've heard these concerns, I could take you to a steak house for dinner! The content for your blog is the heart of the program and is not something to create lightly or just think about when you need a new topic. Writing blog posts is hard work, but it is work that will pay off by increasing your visibility—and visitors—online.

Effective bloggers, like news publishers, consider their content regularly and create an *editorial calendar* for posting blog entries. This way, they know exactly what they will write about and post each day. Take time monthly to

Blogging Effectively

- Select engaging topics.
- Include keywords in titles and text.
- Write to inform, entertain, educate, and encourage readers to act.
- Include photos and video links.

prepare a schedule of posts and jot down ideas whenever and wherever you think of them so you're not struggling with writer's block the day you're scheduled to publish a new entry. Creating this schedule will make it much easier to generate new ideas for content and will allow you the time you need to research your topics.

Having an editorial calendar will enable you to delegate writing responsibilities to multiple bloggers. Engaging multiple voices will attract more visitors because each writer will appeal to a different segment of your market. It's like offering multiple floor plans in your community— some people want a traditional two-story home, some a one-story ranch, some want a first-floor master or in-law arrangement. The company president, vice president of sales and marketing, and sales agents will add an interesting mix of voices and expertise to your blog. If nobody in your company has the skill or time to write, hire a professional social media and blogging company to write and publish for you, but make sure they write original content specifically for you and about your communities. You don't want to duplicate content, or even worse, violate copyright law. If you can have only one blogger, you still can appeal to a variety of buyers by varying the topics you write about; it just may require more research.

Blog Topics

Whether you have one blogger or many responsible for writing your blog content, you should publish content on a variety of topics each month to keep your readers engaged and to expand the keywords you are targeting in the search engines. Write about

- industry-related news;
- media-covered events, news, or trends;
- local area events;
- awards your company has earned;
- charities you support; and
- your products, specials, and incentives.

Be the first company to talk about a particular product, event, or home feature. You want to be the leading expert in your field and in your market. The best way to do that is to publish a wealth of information about a variety of subjects relevant to your industry. You can do this without constantly promoting yourself, which will turn off most consumers.

If you are always promoting yourself, your visitors will not want to keep coming back. They will get tired of the same old sales pitch and begin to ignore your content. A good rule of thumb is for every four blog posts you write, only one should be about your company or product. In other words, write three posts about the industry, a local event, or a holiday for each one about your company, new community, model, or incentive. Using this strategy will expand your keywords, enhance your credibility, and keep people engaged and interested.

Make your posts informal, conversational, fun, and entertaining. Write about topics of interest locally, current events, and upcoming holidays. Write in the first person to demonstrate your credibility and knowledge about your subject so you are viewed as the expert in your area. This will also help the reader connect with your post. Use proper grammar and spelling and avoid using texting abbreviations and industry jargon. At the same time, allow your bloggers' personality to shine through. You don't want to use the same "corporate voice" you would in a press release or advertisement. After you write your blog post, go back and edit it to include keywords and anchor text for links to your website so you feed the search engines. Figures 4.1 and 4.2 show sample blogs with effective content.

Topics for Blogging

- Your local market and local area
- Industry issues
- Local events
- Local historic sites or celebrity homes
- Upcoming holidays
- Legislation (exercise caution with this one or any that refer to politics or religion)
- Area amenities
- Home features
- Community amenities
- Awards your company has earned
- Company staff members
- Testimonials and positive customer feedback
- New products and community openings
- Specials and incentives

Go to Google and search for "blog post topics" to complete this list.

Blogging Schedule

With the recommended eight posts per month, you can steadily build your content so the search engines regularly visit your blog for new material to index. Remember, each post adds a new page to be indexed. Posting regularly will improve your SERP and drive more traffic to your website. A well-built blog with a consistent schedule and well-written, keyword-rich content will become a top referral source to your website in a month or two.

Intuitive Navigation

Although you have to think about your blog's content similarly to your website's, the navigation will be different. In

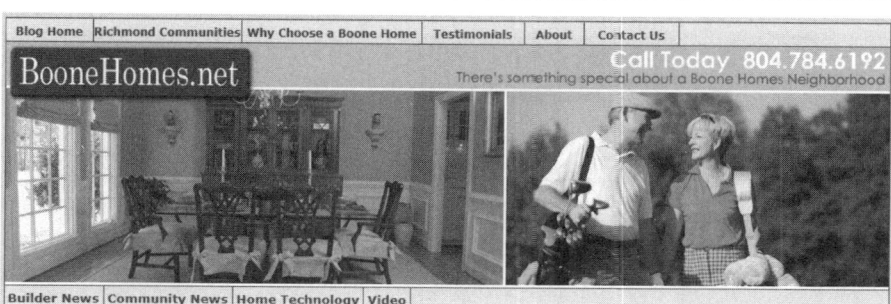

Blog Home | Richmond Communities | Why Choose a Boone Home | Testimonials | About | Contact Us

BooneHomes.net

Call Today 804.784.6192
There's something special about a Boone Homes Neighborhood

Builder News | Community News | Home Technology | Video

New Magical River Front Park

June 7th, 2011 by Chris Parks

"And they lived happily ever after…." if that had been the end of the story. In the case of Tarrington on the James, a community of luxury homes in Richmond, the dream is continuing to be built. The newest phase of this dream is the new river front park following the James River that is now open to the residents of Tarrington on the James. Just imagine a nice stroll in the park that will relax the senses, realign the lucky stars and transition you from the busy day to an organic walk into nature. The private neighborhood park has paths and seating along the river front and can sooth the worries of even the most troubled day.

The elegant new home neighborhood of Tarrington on the James has been one of the most desirable places to live in Richmond since the first new home sold. The entrance to the community speaks luxury; the views speak beauty; the sidewalks, playground, pool and pavilion speak family; and the private wooded home sites speak relaxation. Even the most professional business people can find refuge in this stately new home neighborhood conveniently located in Midlothian's Robious corridor. All this married with award-winning architecture and award-winning schools and you have a combination that is sure to be sought after. Read the rest of this entry »

Tags: custom home builder, new homes, New homes Richmond, richmond custom new homes, Richmond Home builder, richmond virginia, Tarrington on the James
Posted in Builder News, Community News, Richmond | 1 Comment »

Richmond New Home Leadership

June 1st, 2011 by Chris Parks

The history of Richmond is deep, colorful and diverse. Patrick Henry and his speech in Saint John's Church and many more events have shaped the resolve and view of many Richmonders. If the past is any indication of where the future lies, Richmond will be at the forefront of innovation and leadership.

Boone Homes, a Richmond home builder, has a rich philosophy of improvement, innovation and leadership in the new home industry. Like the resolve, detail and delivery invested in Patrick Henry's speech, every detail of a home is planned out in advance and executed completely. Boone Homes has internalized innovation and led the way by building all their homes with ENERGY STAR® features that save home owners more than 38 percent in heating and cooling costs. The detail showcased in every home has been rigorously planned by a staff architect who has won multiple awards in design. Read the rest of this entry »

Tags: Building a New Home, building homes, New homes Richmond va, private new homes, private real estate, richmond custom homes, richmond luxury homes, richmond new homes, richmond real estate
Posted in Builder News, Community News, Richmond | No Comments »

Search

[   ] [Search]

Recent Posts

» New Magical River Front Park
» Richmond New Home Leadership
» Your Greatest Asset: Energy Efficient Richmond New Homes
» 3.5 Virtues of Richmond New Homes with a First Floor Study
» Larger Richmond New Homes, Less Energy

Social Media

Subscribe

Enter your email address:

[   ]

[Subscribe]

Delivered by FeedBurner

Archives

» June 2011
» May 2011
» April 2011
» March 2011
» February 2011
» January 2011
» December 2010
» November 2010
» October 2010
» September 2010
» August 2010
» July 2010
» June 2010
» May 2010
» April 2010
» March 2010
» February 2010
» January 2010
» December 2009
» November 2009

FIGURE 4.1

Boone Homes Blog

Note the variety of information on this page. (Reprinted with permission from Boone Homes, Richmond, Virginia)

FIGURE 4.2 **S & A Homes Blog**

S & A Homes regularly publishes of a variety of content in different voices. (Reprinted with permission from S & A Homes, State College, Pennsylvania)

both cases, users must be able to navigate easily to locate what they want after two to three clicks. A typical builder's website provides information about the company, homes, and communities. Blog content should be similarly categorized so that readers can filter, search for, and find what they are seeking.

Before creating a blog, write an outline of topics or *blog categories*. These "parent" categories will become the top navigation of the blog. Limit them to seven or fewer topics. Each category can also have "children" or subcategories. Here's how Traton Homes of Atlanta categorized its blog topics:

- Home
- News
- Locations
  - Cherokee
  - Cobb
  - North Fulton
  - Paulding
  - South Fulton
- Incentives
- Videos
- Contact Us

Creating Your First Monthly Editorial Calendar

Creating your first monthly editorial calendar for your blog will be easy with these writing prompts:

1. Introduce the blog.
2. Discuss a hot new home feature like home automation.
3. Talk about a local community event near one of your communities.
4. Publish your current or upcoming incentive.
5. Blog about an upcoming holiday.
6. Explain the features of your most popular plan or community amenities.
7. Talk about a local place of interest near one of your communities.
8. Talk about how your home lives (bonus room uses, for example).

Other categories you might want to include are Events, Press Releases (your own), In the News (stories about your company in other media), Testimonials, and Promotions.

Notice how Traton Homes includes navigation both at the top and right side of the page (fig. 4.3). The navigation is easy to find and understand, whether the web visitor generally searches from the top navigation, the side navigation, or the search bar. When you post a blog entry, you should list it under only one category or subcategory so you don't confuse people or the search engines.

Attractive Design

Your blog will be one of the most heavily used sources for your Internet marketing collateral so it must be attractive. With a professionally crafted

FIGURE
4.3
Traton Homes Blog Navigation
You can easily find information on where Traton builds, watch videos, and read news and other nformation on the company's blog. (Reprinted with permission from Traton Homes, Marietta, Georgia)

brand image, you will gain a competitive edge, or at least level the playing field. If you are a small-volume builder competing in a market with larger national or regional companies, for example, having a great looking and effective blog can enlarge your company's image. Conversely, if you are a large national builder trying to compete with a local leader, your blog design can emphasize a local message. So whether you are a large builder, a small-volume builder, a custom builder, a remodeler, or you play another role in the housing industry, a fresh, clean, professionally designed blog will make a positive impression on consumers.

Blogging software and platforms allow for a wide range of designs, similar to traditional websites. If you build your own self-hosted blog, you can have almost any design you want. Each blog platform has benefits and limitations. You can get design ideas by looking at blogs in other industries (figs. 4.4–4.5).

Personalities Inc. Blog Page

FIGURE 4.4

This cool-looking site includes video, huge pictures, and many fun elements.

Functionality ("the coolness factor")

Blogs have some inherent functionality built in and you can easily add more features. They are also easy to manage when they are built properly. All blogs allow categories, will display navigation on both sides of a page, show posts in reverse chronological order, and support RSS feeds. Your blog visitors can subscribe to your RSS feed and receive an e-mail message each time you publish a new post or they can add your RSS feed to their feed reader, a website or other tool where they go to see all their RSS feed streams.

In addition, some blog platforms, like a self-hosted WordPress blog, allow developers to add plug-ins for advanced functionality. Plug-ins are

 Stella Blog Page

The blog for this eclectic women's store demonstrates its unique products and artsy atmosphere. (Reprinted with permission from Stella, Evanston, Illinois)

modules of functionality, or code, you can install on a blog to enhance its capabilities. Go to http://wordpress.org/extend/plugins/ to see and download plug-ins. mRELEVANCE uses plug-ins for photo galleries, contact forms, SEO tools, and other features. Because WordPress is *open source,* any skilled web developer can revise its code to enhance blog and plug-in functionality. Installing and configuring a plug-in generally will cost less—in time and money—than if you built the same or similar functionality from scratch.

Effectiveness

The goals for your blog are slightly different than those for your website. Although the ultimate goal of both sites is to attract customers to your sales centers, your blog should specifically aim to attract the search engines, increase the number of searches your website and blog appear in for targeted keywords, and increase traffic to your website. If you build it correctly, your blog will become a top referral source for your website and drive more traffic to your website than other referring sources will. If you blog effectively–using keywords and anchor text–both your website and blog should appear when you enter your keywords in the Google search engine or check your website's ranking in the search engines with SEO tools like Rank Checker.

As the search engines index each blog post, depending on the blog platform you use, your website can get more link juice for the keywords you've used in your anchor text. The search engines will index your site using those keywords and your blog and website will appear in more and more SERPs.

Blog Platforms

There are several different platforms to choose from when deciding how to build your blog. Many are free and easy to set up so you can start blogging right away. Among the free platforms, I like Word-Press, Blogger, and realestatesiteshub.com. You can go to any of these websites, create an account, and set up your blog. Although each one allows you to build a blog quickly and easily and host it for free, each has limitations. For example, links to your main website in your WordPress.com posts will not improve your website's relevance in the search engines because WordPress.com does not send link juice with outbound links. WordPress.com also limits plug-ins, which constrains design and functionality. Although you can pay for more functionality and features on your WordPress.com site, you still might not get everything you want. The major benefit of a WordPress.com site is its quick and easy setup.

Set up a free blog on WordPress.com

If you don't currently have a blog and want to set up a free wordpress.com blog, follow the instructions below and begin blogging:

1. Go to http://www.wordpress.com.
2. Click the Get Started button.
3. Enter a simple name for your blog (your name, if available).
4. Enter a username that you will remember (your name, if available).
5. Enter a password you won't forget, and confirm.
6. Enter your e-mail address.
7. Click the Sign Up button.
8. Check your In box for the confirmation e-mail with an activation link.
9. Click the activation link and you will have a new blog!
10. Update your profile, publish a blog post, and become familiar with the easy back end of WordPress.

Google's free blogging platform, Blogger.com, on the other hand, is more complicated to use and administer. Unlike WordPress, it sends link juice with your anchor text, so it is more SEO friendly than WordPress.com. My company sometimes creates Blogger blogs as secondary or tertiary blogs to repurpose content with links to a main website or blog.

A third option, realestatesiteshub.com, a free site I created for the industry, is a self-hosted WordPress blog for builders and other companies to create their blogs. Although it is also free, it offers more flexibility than WordPress or Blogger: it sends link juice for SEO, you can add more plug-ins and functionality, and it is easy to use. As with the other free platforms, however, you do not own your blog and you are subject to the system's limitations and the rules of the company that runs the site.

A better option than a free blog is a self-hosted WordPress blog. Go to http://www.WordPress.org (instead of WordPress.com) and click the download button to install the prewritten code into your web hosting environment. Although the code and most of the plug-ins are free, you need a hosting company, which will charge a monthly fee. This option provides you with maximum control of your blog. Most companies hire a professional web development company to download the most current version of WordPress, install it in their hosting environment, design and build a custom blog theme, and maintain the application. This is the option we recommend, and the primary option we implement for our clients.

Self-hosting a WordPress blog allows you to control the design template, plug-ins, search engine optimization, and

Really Simple Syndication

Really Simple Syndication (RSS) is a feature that blogs and news sites use to proactively distribute their content to other sites or directly to users. You can set up or burn an RSS feed of your sites, such as your website and blog, to feed other sites. Subscribers can follow the content on sites through their RSS feeds by: (1) using an *RSS feed reader,* available on websites or smartphones or (2) subscribing to an e-mail version of the RSS feed. RSS feed readers are today's newspapers. You can surf the Internet to find websites and blogs from which you want to receive updates and add them to your RSS feed reader to see all of your news in one place.

Most sites that offer an RSS feed show an icon for you to click to subscribe. Ask your visitors, friends, and others in your network or sphere of influence to subscribe to your feed. E-mail your contacts list and ask them to subscribe. The RSS feed is a great way to syndicate your feed and pique interest, but you have to promote the feed for people to use it.

WordPress and most other blog platforms incorporate built-in feed-burning capabilities. Simply add "/feed/" (without the quotes) to your blog's URL and you will see the feed. If your blog does not have this feed or if you want advanced feed capabilities, you can burn your feed using Google's feedburner by logging in to your Google account and going to http://feedburner.google.com.

advanced functionality, and enables customization and scale-up as your company grows. By controlling your blog's SEO, design, and content, you truly own your blog. The application is free to download and open source, which means that every line of code may be edited. If you don't have the expertise to do it, you can hire a person to install, configure, and customize, while preserving the inherent blogging functionality (like categories, posting, and RSS feeds).

Beyond SEO

Whether to build your blog as part of the main company website, as a separate website, or as your main website depends on variables unique to your company and its goals. Consider these questions to determine which of the three options to choose:

Subscribing to and Burning an RSS Feed

Subscribe to a feed:
1. Go to http://www.mrelevance.com/feed/.
2. Follow the instructions in the Subscribe Now! box.

Burn a feed using feedburner:
1. Create a blog and a Google account.
2. Go to http://feedburner.google.com.
3. Type the URL of your blog in the "Burn a feed right this instant" box and click next.
4. Approve or edit the title and the feedburner address for the feed.
5. Your feed is now active.
6. Go into the account you created and review the settings under the Optimize and Publicize tabs to configure your feed.

1. Do you want a single online portal for information about your company or many gateways?
2. Who will manage the blog and what are their capabilities?
3. Do you have a website that already captures leads effectively but needs more traffic?
4. Are you concerned more about SEO or brand identity or are they equal concerns?

Generally, locating your blog on a site separate from your website and in a different hosting account is the most effective SEO strategy. The search engines see the blog as a separate website and give link juice to the links from the blog to the website. Your SERPs would also potentially include two links from your website and two from your blog in the top 10 results that appear on the first page of search results. However, SEO usually isn't the only consideration. Sometimes a company's website is so weak that a blog can supplant it. In other cases, a company's website is robust enough without a blog. Another option is to have the website and blog hosted separately but to design the blog to look like the website. You can certainly help quench the search engines' thirst for new content with SEO juice you capture by separating the blog from the website, but the practical payoff might not warrant the additional work of maintaining a separate blog. Discuss various options with your Internet marketing team and the professionals who create, design, and manage websites, blogs, and SEO.

Budgeting for the Blog

Although the software to host a blog might be free, creating, designing, and maintaining it to be search-engine friendly requires time and resources. If a relative builds you a blog using a free platform, it might not cost you any money but it may not be effective either. People often forget that even though the base software is free, you need to invest time to set up the blog to

- be search engine friendly;
- be professionally designed in a custom template; and
- remain within the blog architecture so that the inherent blog functionality remains intact.

However, you should be able to get a professionally created blog on a free blog platform, using a standard blog theme, for $500–$1,500. This is your "entry-level" blog. It will have limited capabilities and limited results. Most self-hosted blogs our company builds cost $3,500–$7,500, depending on the intricacies of the design and the desired functionality. We have built self-hosted custom-themed blogs for as little $2,500. We also have created fully functional custom-designed blogs for more than $30,000. These are integrated with back-office software and replace a main website.

Once the blog is built, you need someone to maintain the editorial calendar; write, edit, and proofread the content; moderate comments; and optimize posts for the search engines. These activities can cost $1,200–$2,500 per month. This money is well worth the investment to have a foundation for your social media program and connect and automate updates to other social media sites.

Other Groups' Blogs

In addition to having your own properly built and self-hosted blog, posting content on other blogs will increase the number of sites that drive traffic to your website. After you have written eight posts for a month, look for other blogs that allow users to post content as guest bloggers. This strategy adds third-party credibility to your links, content, and website. It also strengthens your online brand position by adding relevant links back to your website.

If you become a guest blogger, don't duplicate posts on multiple sites. The search engines like original content. Instead of redundant blog posts, write unique *teasers* to a blog post to put on other blogs. Vary which blogs you place the full content on and which ones you use for the teasers. This strategy keeps your content circulating and your search-engine credibility growing in multiple places. You can repurpose a blog post if you refresh it with at least 40% revised or new text.

Another strategy for keeping your company's name circulating on the web and populating the search engines is to comment on others' blog posts where the blog permits this. Writing a positive comment about another writer's article or commenting on a post builds your network and name recognition. Some blogs will even allow you to add a link to your comments. You can also ask other bloggers to guest blog on your site. Ask your preferred lender or design center manager if they want to write for your blog.

Although you should always allow readers to comment on your blog posts, you or someone in your company must screen comments for propriety and remove spam. Screening your comments, or moderating your blog, means reading, approving—or possibly editing or deleting—comments before they are published. Having comments on your blog increases the interaction on your blog and may encourage readers to interact with you. Readers will not comment often, but when they offer constructive comments, they can strengthen your blog and increase its visibility. However, publishing unmoderated comments with links to irrelevant or inappropriate content can prompt Google to blacklist your blog.

Blogging Mistakes to Avoid

- Posting too much self-promotional content compared with other content. Your blog should not just advertise, it should inform, educate, or entertain readers.
- Blogging about politics or religion.
- Neglecting your blog. If eight posts per month are too many, consider starting with four and increasing the pace over time.
- Duplicating content. You can revise and repurpose, but don't repeat or Google will penalize your blog.
- Complicating management with poor design and setup. Hire professionals who understand and specialize in developing a blog that is easy to manage and update.

Automating Social Media

In *Social Media for Home Builders 2.0: It's Easier Than You Think*[4], Carol Flammer offers six rules for interacting with others using social media:

1. Complete your profiles.
2. Engage others.
3. Use the right tools to build your sites correctly.
4. Engage and interact with the right people.
5. Have a plan for content.
6. Link it all together.

Your blog will increase SEO exponentially by automatically streaming content to social media sites which in turn feed the search engines. You can automate status updates and regular teasers with links to your blog as you post new content. How to do this is explained later in this chapter. You will learn, for each site, how that site can receive the content from your blog to update your status or post.

Microblogs

A microblog, as its name implies, is a miniblog. It differs from other blogs in that it is much smaller than a regular blog. A post on a microblog could be a short sentence, a phrase, an image, a link, or embedded video. Twitter is a microblog. Tweets, the updates or messages sent through Twitter, are limited to 140 characters but you can include links to other sites and to content such as web pages, images, and videos. When you join Twitter and register your account you should create your profile with a photo or avatar, information about yourself that includes links to your website, and a background image that demonstrates your brand. Figures 4.6 and 4.7 show two different Twitter accounts. Each one has a custom-designed background, keyword-rich tweets with links, and shows interaction among Twitter members.

Your goal using Twitter and other microblogs is to find people that you

What to Include in Your Profile

1. Company name
2. Company objectives, mission statement, or both
3. Market segments you serve
4. Promotions or incentives you offer
5. Your Unique Selling Proposition (USP)

FIGURE 4.6 **Atlanta Real Estate Forum Twitter Microblog**
Notice the custom background and the links with each tweet. (Reprinted with permission from mRELEVANCE LLC)

want to follow, and try to get others to follow you. Your profile on Twitter is what people will review to determine if they will want to follow your stream of tweets, your stream of 140-character updates. Besides your photo or avatar and the information you enter in your profile, other Twitter users will read your stream of tweets and the list of your followers to determine whether to follow you. Use thoughtful keyword-rich tweets and links to your website, in your tweets. Encourage followers to interact with you. Although you will not be able to use anchor text in your tweets, tweeting with keyword-rich content and posting links and images will help SEO and SMO.

You can pitch your messages and stories directly to the media, Realtors in your local market who sell your homes, and other referral sources using Twitter. You can interact with people one-on-one, or broadcast your message to all of your followers, but think about Twitter and the other microblogs as vehicles for directly reaching referral sources and indirectly reaching consumers. A customer will rarely contact you

FIGURE 4.7 **Boone Homes Twitter Microblog**
Your tweets should encourage *retweets* and other interaction. (Reprinted with permission from Boone Homes, Richmond, Virginia)

directly using Twitter. But a journalist might contact you for a quote in an industry publication or write a story about your company. A Realtor might bring a buyer to your sales center. Use the search functions on the microblogs to find people to follow and followers to build your network.

Your tweets should have focus, make sense, and be targeted for maximum impact. As Carol says, "They don't need to be personal, but they should have personality." In addition to building the network of followers, you should strive to get people to retweet your tweets to their network of Twitter followers. This is viral marketing using social media. Once you have enough followers to yield interaction, try to engage them further by asking open-ended questions.

Automating Tweets
You can automate your microblogging strategy using tools to automatically tweet or update other microblogging sites with posts from your main blog. These tools will tweet with links to the full entry on your blog.

Developers are constantly creating new automation tools but Twitter continually changes as well, so monitor what's happening with your Twitter account to ensure the tools you use are working. I have found that they all need to be reset periodically when Twitter makes a change or your blog is updated. You can install one of many Twitter plug-ins on

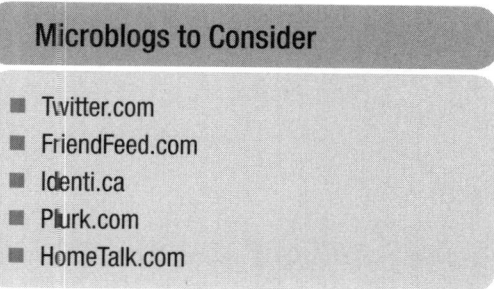

Microblogs to Consider

- Twitter.com
- FriendFeed.com
- Identi.ca
- Plurk.com
- HomeTalk.com

your WordPress blog by visiting the WordPress plug-in site and searching for "Twitter plug-ins." I have used WordPress for Twitter and Twitter Tools. The tool I use most often, however, is Google's FeedBurner. In your FeedBurner account on the "Publicize" tab is a "Socialize" link in the left navigation (fig. 4.8). This page will let you enter your Twitter

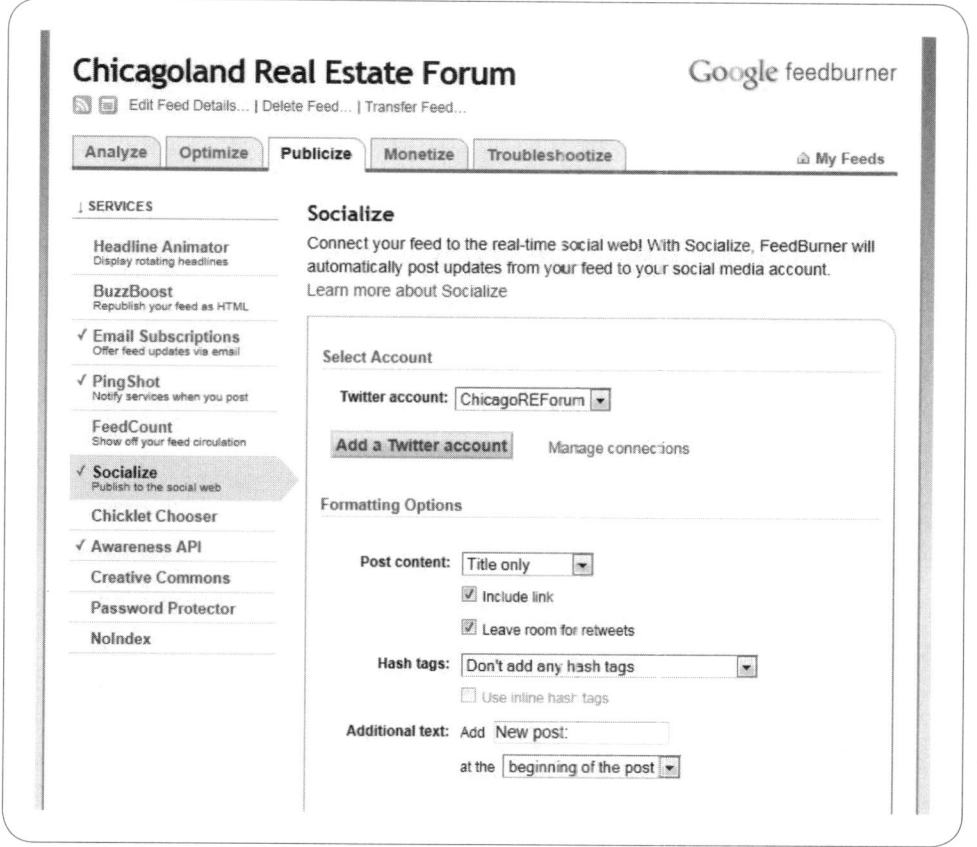

FIGURE 4.8 **Chicagoland Real Estate Forum FeedBurner**

Setting up Google FeedBurner to tweet (Reprinted with permission from mRELEVANCE LLC)

handle and password and will tweet for you when something new hits your RSS feed. This is my favorite method because we already use Feed-Burner for the RSS feed from the blog. Of course, it probably does not hurt to use Google tools to strengthen SEO.

There are also tools available to help you manage your Twitter account(s) so that you can effectively follow people, use multiple accounts for different purposes, schedule your tweets to post ahead of time and organize your streams to manage them. Two of these tools are HootSuite and TweetDeck. They allow you to monitor the tweets of people you follow, organize people into groups, categorize their tweets, and schedule your

> ### Link from Twitter
>
> Leave space for a link to your website or blog within the 140-character limit for tweets to make your Twitter page a top-10 referral site for your blog or website. Your Twitter profile, over time, also will become a SERP link for your name and your company's.

tweets. Both of these tools help me monitor the many Twitter accounts I manage for my clients and my personal accounts, which include:

- @mRELEVANCE, for tweets about my company, the mRELE-VANCE blog tweets, and retweets of technical ideas I find online
- @MitchLevinson3, my personal blog, MitchLevinson.com, where I interact about my love of fantasy football, sports, and other personal interests
- @mlcFlatFeeRealty, about real estate sales
- @ChicagolandRealEstateForum, about the Chicagoland real estate market and where the blog we run tweets blog posts and links.

TweetDeck and HootSuite save time so I can focus on writing effective tweets for each account.

Social Networks

Social Networks are sites where people go to interact with other people. Some of these sites are strictly for business networking and others are designed for professional and social interaction. Although there are a lot of social networks, the four most popular social networks our industry uses are Facebook, LinkedIn, ActiveRain, and RealtyJoin. The newest one, Google+, has also begun to build momentum and gain marketshare.

Facebook

Facebook is the website most people think of first when they hear the term "social networking." More than 750 million active users and more than 70% of Americans are on Facebook. They have an average of 130 friends each. It is the largest social networking site. The site began as a tool for personal communication, and you now can integrate Facebook into your corporate marketing and communication strategy. As you create your Facebook strategy, keep in mind that Facebook users want to interact with people, not companies.

Let's face it, people do not go to Facebook to buy a house. Potential buyers research your reputation to see how you interact with your customers and to look for coupons and discounts. Facebook users want to interact with people, not companies; they want to know you are real. People do business with people they like and who are like them. Encourage users to visit, and *Like* your page by offering them a discount or incentive. When a visitor clicks the Like button on your Facebook page, it is as if they are giving you their endorsement. That "Like" appears on their personal profile for all of their friends to see. If one of their friends is looking for a home, they may find your business page and see their friend's endorsement when they are on their friend's page. Hopefully that will send them to your page, to your website, and then to your sales center. The goal of your Facebook presence is getting people to Like your page, and interact with you on your Facebook wall so their network will find your company. If you get all of this to happen, you become a credible personal referral. You always have a better chance at conversion when handed a personal referral with a credible introduction. Facebook is a great source of these kinds of referrals.

Create a profile on Facebook and then invite people you know to *friend* you. You can keep your personal and business information separate. Give your business page information to your colleagues and your personal profile information to your friends. Adjust your privacy settings so only your personal friends can see your personal contact information. To do this, click Account settings and Privacy settings (under Account) when you are logged into Facebook. Review each setting (there are many), carefully considering what information you will share with which individuals or groups of people. After you create your profile and set it to be safe, build your business page and reach out to local Realtors, friends, and clients through e-mail, phone calls, and other personalized contact to get them to go to your Facebook company page. Some people will Like your page just because you request it. Others may require an incentive, such as an opportunity to win a prize or a discount coupon (fig. 4.9). Following are some ideas for using Facebook effectively:

1. E-mail clients and other referral sources and ask them to go to your company's page and click the Like button. Many people in your network will do this just because you ask them to. The message or e-mail does not matter as much as the fact that you ask for their action. Some of our clients simply send a personal note to their clients, while others send HTML e-mails.

2. Put the Facebook badge and the Like button on your website and blog so your Web visitors can Like your Facebook page from your website (fig 4.10).

3. After your page has 25 fans, go to http://www.facebook.com/user-name and claim a custom URL username (e.g., http://www.facebook.com/mrelevance). You can also do this from the drop-down account management menu on your corporate page. This will allow you to easily promote your Facebook page through a simple link, instead of the default URL Facebook assigns to your profile.

4. Have your web development company build a Facebook website to add to your Facebook business page in an iFrame. For more information about Facebook iFrame Tabs, go to https://developers.facebook.com/blog/post/462/.

FIGURE 4.9 **Acadia Homes Facebook Coupon Example**
Cash offers are a proven strategy to attract users from your Facebook page to your sales center. (Reprinted with permission from Acadia Homes, Atlanta, Georgia)

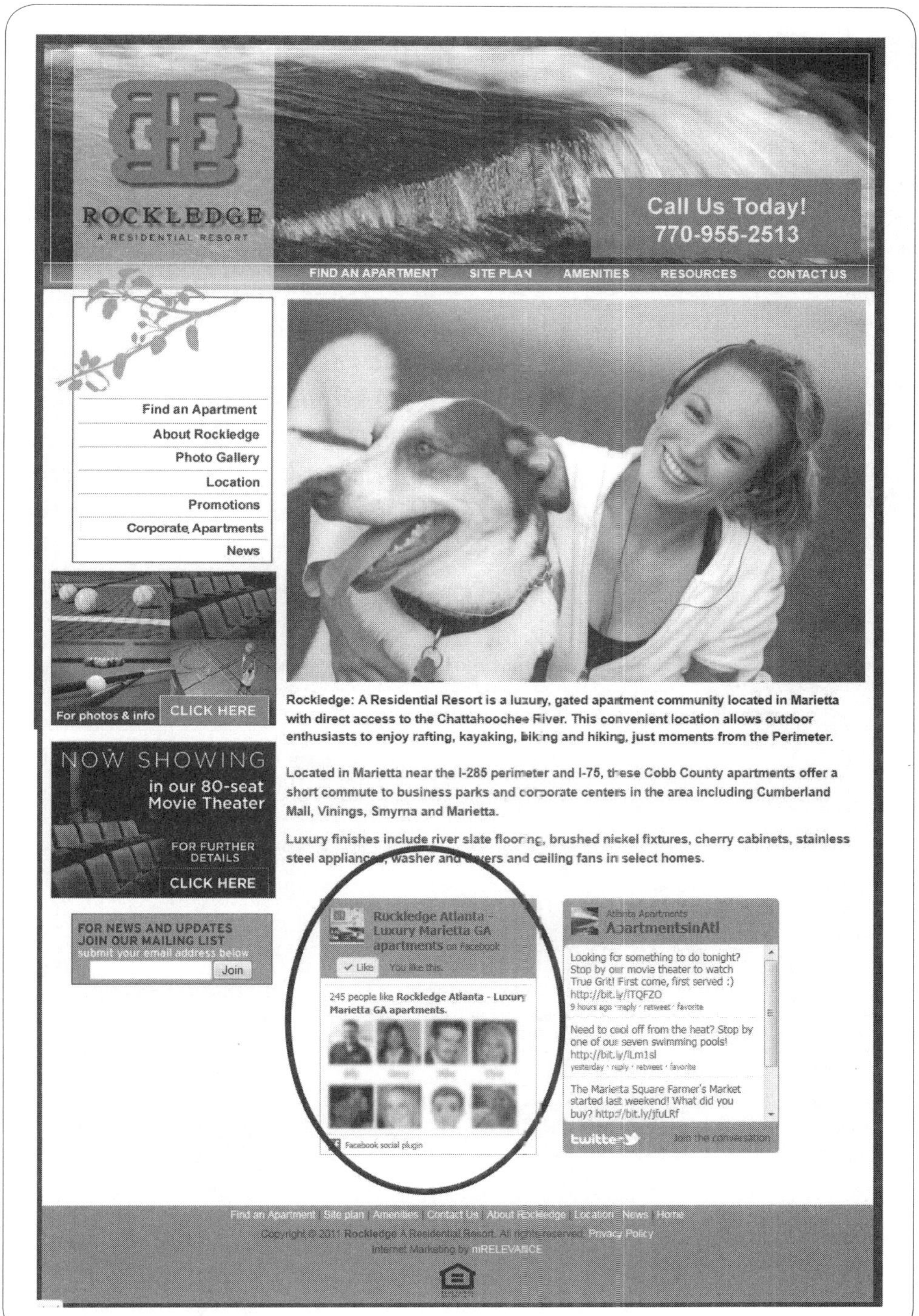

FIGURE 4.10 **Rockledge Facebook Like Button**
Make it easy for visitors to Like you on Facebook with a button on your website. (Reprinted with permission from Ceebraid Signal, Stamford, Connecticut)

Automating Facebook Status

Just like your blog automatically publishes to Twitter, you can set up your blog to update your business page on Facebook. Some web-based tools automatically post a teaser and a link to your blog whenever you publish a new entry. NetworkedBlogs, RSSGraffiti, and Notes are three of these tools. You can search for these applications on Facebook or Google to learn how to add them to your blog or Facebook business page. Monitor this connectivity because, like Twitter connections, changes often break the connection so you must reset these tools.

5. Link to your website, blog, and other online tools to your profile and include them in posts.
6. Create a strategy for posting content and an editorial calendar that will keep your Facebook page fresh. Use automated feeds and manually publish regular updates with open-ended questions and interactive content.

   S & A Homes has an effective Facebook page (fig. 4.11). Company officials note that most of their new Likes come from home buyers shortly after they have signed a contract. Buyers review

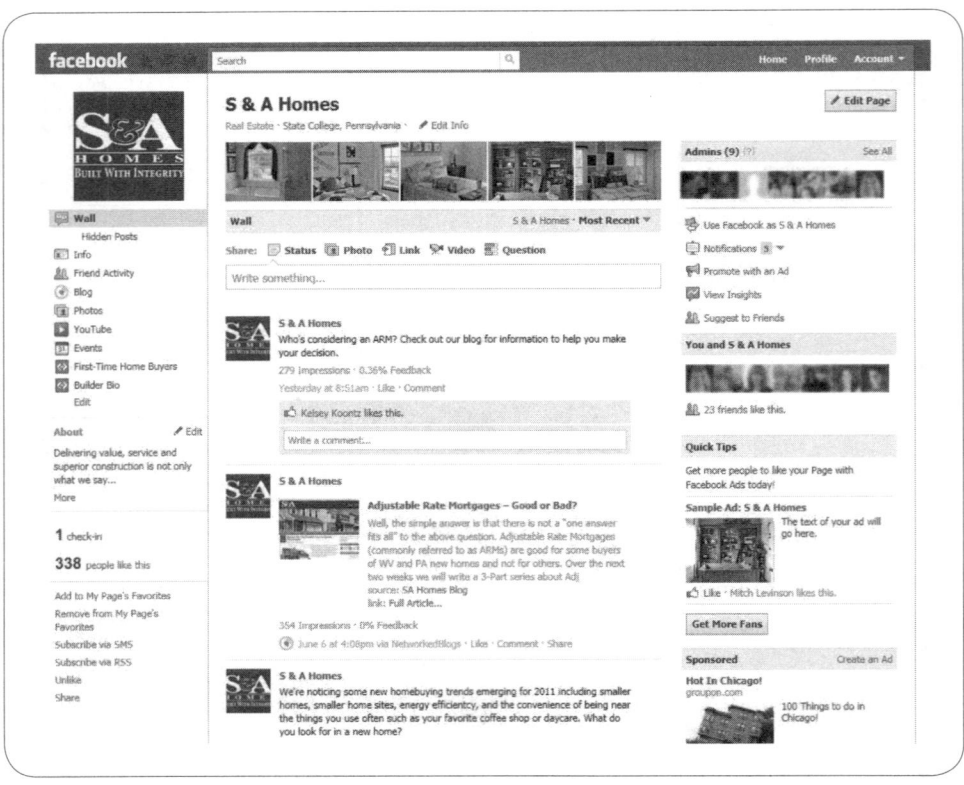

FIGURE 4.11   **S & A Homes Facebook Page Example**
S & A Homes keeps its Facebook page fresh with manual and automatic updates. (Reprinted with permission from S & A Homes, State College, Pennsylvania)

Facebook in making buying decisions, but don't offer an endorsement until they have signed a contract.

LinkedIn

Similar to Facebook but designed for professional networking, LinkedIn is your online Rolodex and a new network marketing program. Whereas Facebook is the preferred site for people to interact socially with friends, LinkedIn is the networking site for those seeking professional connections, visibility, and career information. You might find clients and customers on LinkedIn, but the site is more useful for doing research on prospective home buyers. Similar to Facebook, however, people on LinkedIn want to connect, network, and interact with you personally, even if you represent a company. Complete your profile, including work history and resume; connect with your past and current colleagues, classmates, and associates; and join Groups relevant to your professional interests. You can ask and answer questions in group discussions to increase your visibility and share your expertise.

To effectively incorporate LinkedIn in your Internet marketing, use keywords to complete your profile when you post comments so other users can find you or your expertise when they search their LinkedIn Rolodex. As with Twitter and Facebook, you can update your LinkedIn status using your blog by adding an application that will display your blog's RSS feed. In addition to automatic updates, you should manually update LinkedIn once or twice a month on your professional activities.

ActiveRain

ActiveRain is a social networking site specifically for the real estate industry. Builders, Realtors, mortgage brokers, and others in the real estate industry use ActiveRain to connect with each other. Real estate agents dominate the site so it is a terrific place to beef up your outreach to co-op agents and communicate with them as a niche.

After you create a profile on ActiveRain, you can communicate with others and create your own blog on the site. You must pay a monthly fee to post your blog publicly (so it appears in search engine results) or if you want your ActiveRain account integrated with your Facebook and Twitter accounts.

You can interact with other ActiveRain users by commenting on their blog posts, joining a group or groups, or starting a group. The more you use and interact with the site the more points you earn to raise your profile's visibility.

RealtyJoin

RealtyJoin is a new real-estate-industry-specific social networking site designed with investors in mind. Industry participants connect and interact based on specific deals or projects. Investors, lenders, brokers, trade contractors, and others in the industry use RealtyJoin as a catalyst for finding their next deal. The site offers users a free blog and the opportunity to join groups and interact with other real estate professionals.

Google+

Google+ had more than 2 million users during a two-week "invitation only" launch and 25 million after one month. It took Facebook and Twitter two years to get 2 million users.

Google+ has incorporated the concept of "Circles," for categorizing your connections. For example, you may have a circle of friends, a circle of business associates, a circle of prospects or clients, and a circle of industry professionals you want to keep up with. The concept of circles allows you to post updates and interact with people in the circle you choose. Google+ has also announced plans to index updates and other new material in the search engine. Google+ may be positioning itself as the most indexed and SEO-friendly social networking site. Not mainstream at the time this book was published, Google+ still has to prove that it can get regular visitors to the site and interacting with others once the novelty of the site wears off.

Social Networking Sites

Following are some of the social networking sites. Wikipedia lists others (http://en.wikipedia.org/wiki/List_of_social_networking_websites).

- Facebook
- LinkedIn
- RealtyJoin
- ActiveRain
- Google+
- Ning
- LiveJournal
- MySpace

A Personal Touch

Although you should automate posting from your blog to your social networking sites, to maximize your effectiveness on the Internet you must interact personally with your friends, contacts, and followers. You should manually update your status, read your feed, and check comments about your posts two to four times per week on all sites. Consider this as you decide which social networking sites to add to your toolbox. Creating profiles and pages and then leaving them dormant will spoil your brand.

Local Search

Location, Location, Location. Because most searches for real estate begin with location criteria, you should create profiles on local sites. Local search allows your company to create a local presence online, be part of the local community, and increase your visibility in the search engines. When your buyers are searching for a new home, they are typically targeting a particular area. Say that area is Chicago and the keyword is "Chicago new homes." Even if the buyer forgets to put the word Chicago in the search box and only searches "new homes," the search engines know where the search originated and adjusts SERPs with websites from that area. Among the sites that have local search, Google Places, Yelp, and Foursquare are the most popular.

Google Places

Google Places is currently the most important local site online because it ties into the other Google applications, like Google Maps. Each location you build in, along with your corporate address, should be added to Google Places and have its own page. To build or verify your *Google Places page* profile go to http://www.google.com/places while you are logged into Google. If your location already exists in Google Places, just click the "Business Owner? Verify" link at the top of the page and follow the instructions to verify your location so you can modify and enhance your profile. The verification process is simple. Google will either call your office phone number or mail a postcard to your physical address. Whichever process you select, you will be given a code to type into your Places page that will verify you are the owner and will allow you to edit the page.

Your Places page offers potential customers a concise overview of your company with rich content that may include videos and photos. You can also add coupons and hours of operation to your page, and your buyers can rate your company and leave testimonials. Sterling Custom Homes of Austin, Texas, has verified its profile. If you Google "Austin custom home builders" the company appears in the search results with a bubble containing the letter "A." If you click the map *widget* next to the list or the bubble, you will enter a virtual storefront with details about the company, including photos, videos, and a customer testimonial (fig. 4.12).

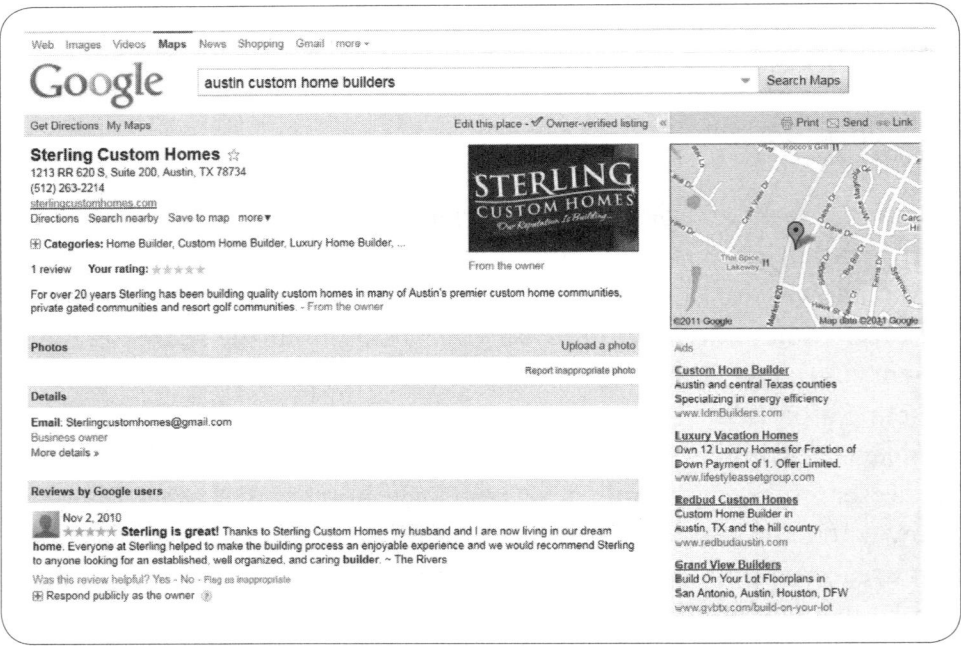

FIGURE 4.12 **Sterling Custom Homes Google Places page**
This full profile includes a positive review. (Reprinted with permission from Sterling Custom Homes, Austin, Texas)

A Google Places page adds to the search index, allows you to add your keywords to another profile, and creates another link to your website from the search engine. The mapping feature is also particularly valuable because Google may not be able to locate new home communities any other way. If the streets are not built and dedicated they may not appear on a map. But don't worry if Google Places maps your location incorrectly. You can manually drag and drop your dot on the map to the proper location when you edit your page.

Local Online Rating Sites

Yelp, the Better Business Bureau (BBB), and other local online rating sites allow

Create a Places Page

1. Go to Google.com/Places.
2. Click on the Get Started button.
3. Locate your business.
4. If you find it, follow these steps:
   - Click to verify your business.
   - Select the "send postcard" option.
   - When the postcard arrives, go to Google.com/Places and type in the code.
   - Edit your Google Places page.

If you don't find your business, click "add a business" and follow the instruction wizard to create your business and profile on Google Places.

customers to rate you online like Google Places. The BBB includes a company profile and a place for customers to write reviews at http://www.bbbonline.com. If your company is a member of the Better Business Bureau, the organization allows you to add a badge to your site to show that you are a member and that you care about and respond to customer complaints.

You can also add your company profile to Yelp (http://www.yelp.com), a popular site for consumers to research and review companies. Yelp and other sites like it provide the ultimate customer testimonial and third-party credibility, so make sure you manage your presence on them effectively. Don't mistakenly believe that neglecting sites with space for customer reviews allows you to avoid unhappy customers. Use these sites to contact unhappy customers and try to rectify problems. If you don't create a company profile on them, a customer can, and then they can write a review. Creating a profile is only a minimum requirement, however, for managing review sites. You should also proactively manage your online reputation by encouraging customers to write positive reviews of your company (fig. 4.13). Your reputation will improve when you skillfully handle neutral or negative feedback.

Actively using local search sites helps you manage your reputation in at least two ways: (1) by building strong positive links and content that is indexed in the search engines before negative information gains link juice; and (2) by answering consumer criticism professionally online so future buyers see that you interact with customers respectfully and deal with problems fairly.

Search Games

Some social networking sites, such as Facebook, have a local search component (http://www.facebook.com/places). You can share your location with friends and find places near your location based on your profile.

Some local search websites, like Foursquare and Gowalla, integrate games with local search. Consumers can "check in" using their smartphone app when they are at a particular location. You earn points whenever you check in on Foursquare. When you check in more often than anyone else, you become that loca-

Build Your Brand with Local Search

1. Google your company.
2. Click every link on the first two pages.
3. Note all local search sites where your company appears.
4. Type a list of local search sites where you will create profiles.

FIGURE 4.13   **A Yelp Page**
Your local search profile should convince buyers to contact you. (Reprinted with permission from
Jude Schmidt Custom Construction, Marengo, Illinois)

tion's "mayor." Businesses may offer an incentive for people who check in,
and sometimes special deals for the mayor. Builders have used these sites to
promote events or provide incentives for people visiting sales centers and
checking in. If you have a Realtor open house, for instance, you can have

a raffle or give a small gift to all the agents who visit and check in. Although there are more effective local search sites, you get a small brand boost with search games.

Online Public Relations

Online public relations websites publish press releases and other information for journalists. They offer opportunities to create referring links for targeted keywords and improve your SEO. Some sites are free and some charge annual, monthly, or per-use fees. You can find fee-free sites with a PR score of 4 or greater, but don't hesitate to pay for those that drive traffic. Some public relations sites are listed in Resources at the back of the book.

Several local markets have their own PR sites, news blogs, and websites where you can place articles and press releases. Consider local newspaper sites and research other options. For example, in Atlanta, we post and blog on Atlanta Daybook and AtlantaRealEstate Forum.com, and in Chicago, on *Chicago Agent* magazine and Chicagoland RealEstateForum.com (figs. 4.14 and 4.15). Of course, we include keywords in the anchor text and, if possible, photos and other images. These sites help build brand awareness and drive traffic to your site.

Photo Sharing and Video Syndication

Just as professional quality photography can entice web visitors to go see your homes in person, poor-quality photos will turn off visitors. Therefore, you should hire a professional photographer to take high-quality photos of your homes and your staff. With a portfolio of professional photos, you can attract users to your website and blog.

In addition, photo sharing sites allow you to create public online albums of your images. After you upload photos, link to them from multiple places and use keywords and metadata to ensure they appear on your SERP for your keywords. These images will appear in an image search in the search engines and provide SEO juice and drive traffic. Although several photo sharing sites send link juice, start with Google's Picasa© Web Album (http://picasaweb.google.com) and Flickr® by Yahoo! (fig. 4.16). These sites index your photos in the image search on the search engines and drive traffic to your website and blog.

Online videos are also valuable Internet marketing collateral. Two of my favorite sites to create video channels with an online profile and

FIGURE 4.14

Gerstad Builders on Chicagoland Real Estate Forum
Effective anchor text and images link users to Gerstad Builders' other sites. (Reprinted with permission from Gerstad Builders, McHenry, Illinois)

upload videos are YouTube (fig 4.17) and MetaCafe. Because the search engines cannot read the content in a video, you must describe or summarize the content of your videos using keywords when you upload them. You also can copy code from the sites to paste into a blog post or on your website so you can stream the video from there. Visitors can click on these videos to visit your channel and also subscribe to it so they can view other videos on the channel.

Even with the convenience of a flip camera, there is no substitute for a professionally created video. Hiring a company to help script a video and having an expert shoot and edit the footage is worth the cost

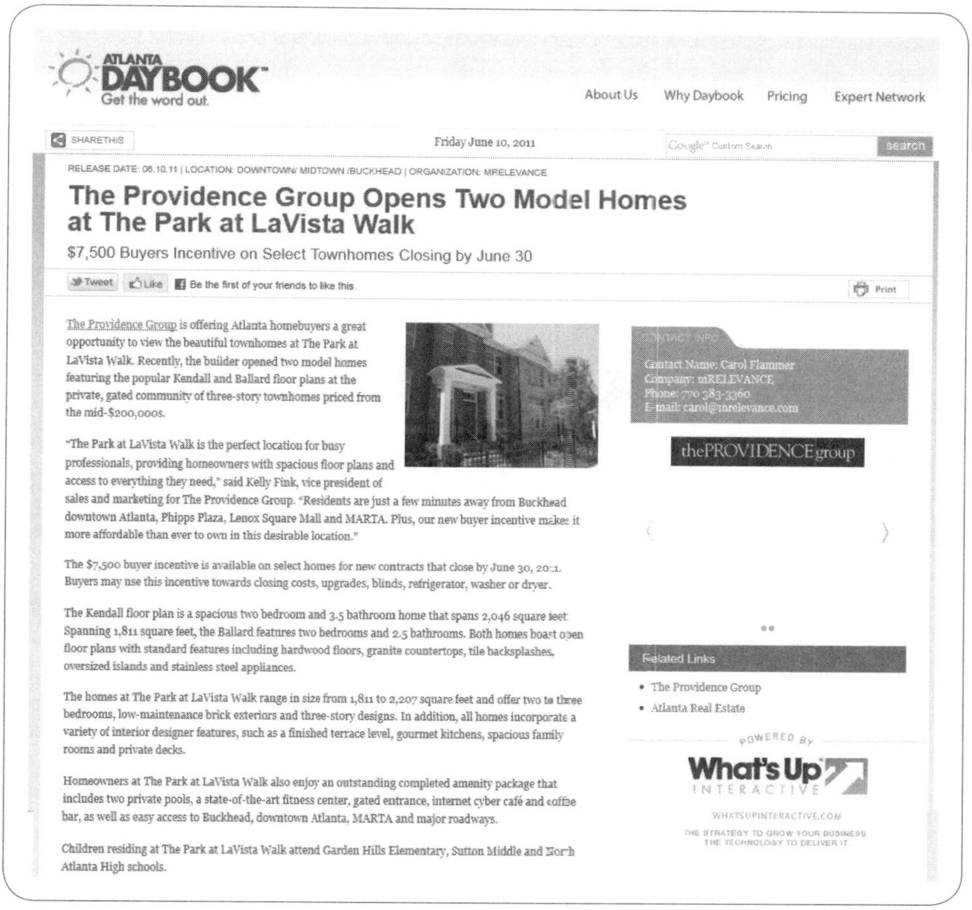
ATLANTA DAYBOOK
Get the word out.
About Us | Why Daybook | Pricing | Expert Network

SHARETHIS | Friday June 10, 2011 | Google Custom Search | search

RELEASE DATE: 06.10.11 | LOCATION: DOWNTOWN/ MIDTOWN /BUCKHEAD | ORGANIZATION: MRELEVANCE

The Providence Group Opens Two Model Homes at The Park at LaVista Walk

$7,500 Buyers Incentive on Select Townhomes Closing by June 30

Tweet | Like | Be the first of your friends to like this. | Print

The Providence Group is offering Atlanta homebuyers a great opportunity to view the beautiful townhomes at The Park at LaVista Walk. Recently, the builder opened two model homes featuring the popular Kendall and Ballard floor plans at the private, gated community of three-story townhomes priced from the mid-$200,000s.

"The Park at LaVista Walk is the perfect location for busy professionals, providing homeowners with spacious floor plans and access to everything they need," said Kelly Fink, vice president of sales and marketing for The Providence Group. "Residents are just a few minutes away from Buckhead downtown Atlanta, Phipps Plaza, Lenox Square Mall and MARTA. Plus, our new buyer incentive makes it more affordable than ever to own in this desirable location."

The $7,500 buyer incentive is available on select homes for new contracts that close by June 30, 2011. Buyers may use this incentive towards closing costs, upgrades, blinds, refrigerator, washer or dryer.

The Kendall floor plan is a spacious two bedroom and 3.5 bathroom home that spans 2,046 square feet. Spanning 1,811 square feet, the Ballard features two bedrooms and 2.5 bathrooms. Both homes boast open floor plans with standard features including hardwood floors, granite countertops, tile backsplashes, oversized islands and stainless steel appliances.

The homes at The Park at LaVista Walk range in size from 1,811 to 2,207 square feet and offer two to three bedrooms, low-maintenance brick exteriors and three-story designs. In addition, all homes incorporate a variety of interior designer features, such as a finished terrace level, gourmet kitchens, spacious family rooms and private decks.

Homeowners at The Park at LaVista Walk also enjoy an outstanding completed amenity package that includes two private pools, a state-of-the-art fitness center, gated entrance, internet cyber café and coffee bar, as well as easy access to Buckhead, downtown Atlanta, MARTA and major roadways.

Children residing at The Park at LaVista Walk attend Garden Hills Elementary, Sutton Middle and North Atlanta High schools.

CONTACT INFO
Contact Name: Carol Flammer
Company: mRELEVANCE
Phone: 770 383-3360
E-mail: carol@mrelevance.com

thePROVIDENCEgroup

Related Links
- The Providence Group
- Atlanta Real Estate

POWERED BY
What's Up INTERACTIVE
WHATSUPINTERACTIVE.COM
THE STRATEGY TO GROW YOUR BUSINESS. THE TECHNOLOGY TO DELIVER IT.

FIGURE 4.15 **Press release on Atlanta Daybook**
Daybook publishes press releases with anchor text. (Reprinted with permission from The Providence Group, Atlanta, Georgia)

when showcasing your models. Professional video can demonstrate the quality of your product, your company, communities, and building process. You can create videos about subjects you write about in your blog.

> **Recording Video**
>
> You can easily and inexpensively record videos with a flip video camera. These cameras cost about $150. When you are ready to upload a video to your YouTube or other online channel, plug the camera into your computer and follow the instructions that automatically start. Most cameras and computers are smart enough to walk you through uploading and completing the metadata for each video on each channel.

Social Bookmarking

You probably have created a *bookmark* for a website or saved it as a *favorite*.

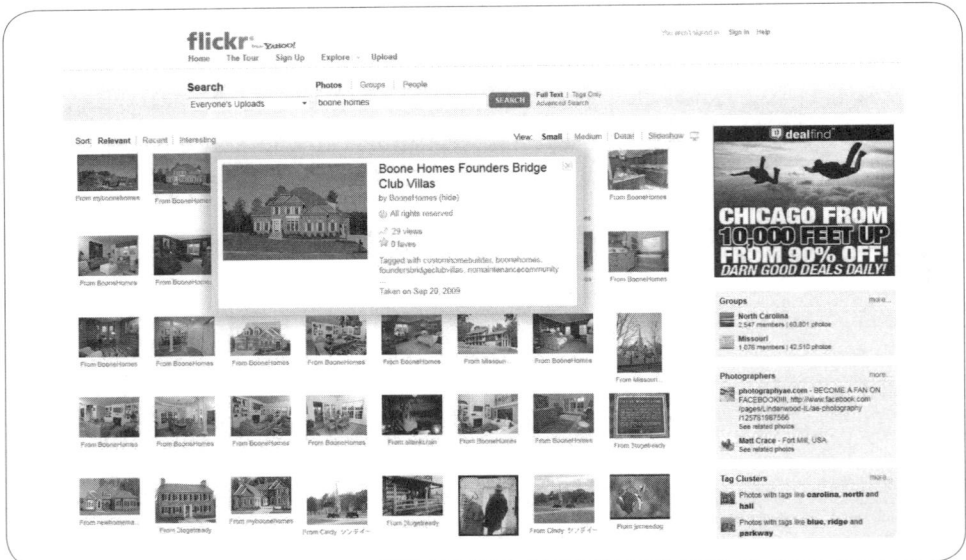

FIGURE 4.16

Boone Homes on Flickr

Boone Homes has tagged its photos so the search engines can find them. (Reprinted with permission from Boone Homes, Richmond, Virginia)

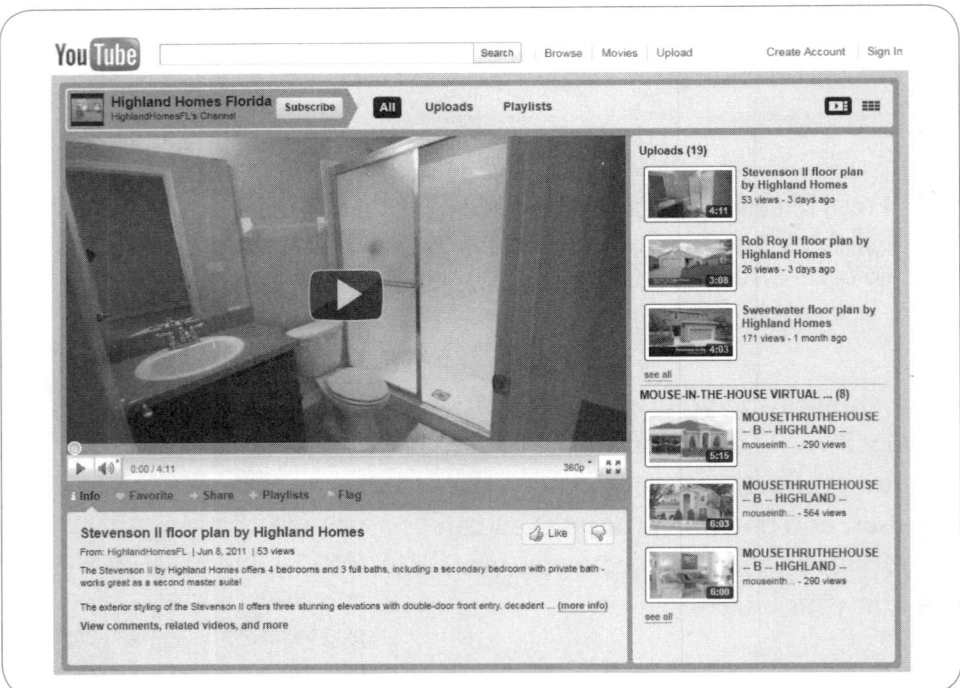

FIGURE 4.17

Highland Homes Florida YouTube channel

Use title tags and descriptions for SEO. (Reprinted with permission from Highland Homes, Lakeland, Florida)

Social bookmarking websites combine bookmarking with social media. You can create an online profile and become friends with others on a bookmarking site, and then save web pages, blog posts, or other online content as favorites for others to see and use. Social bookmarking is an advanced social media and SEO technique, so I would use the other social media tools before trying bookmarking. Here's one way to use social bookmarking: After you publish a blog entry, submit your post to an online bookmarking site. Your goal is to get others in your network to bookmark the post. The more you bookmark other people's content, the more likely they are to like your bookmarks. You should create several bookmarking accounts on different sites and strategically rotate where you bookmark your blog posts. Do not bookmark only your own links in your account because the bookmarking sites will remove your account if you do. I would bookmark three to four posts from other sources for each one from your company. My favorite social bookmarking sites are Digg, StumbleUpon, Delicious, and Reddit. Others sites are listed in the Resources at the back of the book.

Time, Thought, Strategy

Using social media effectively demands more than simply launching a Facebook page or setting up a Twitter account. Your ongoing challenge is to fill up the search engines with positive keyword-rich content about your company that you generate in order to drive traffic back to your website and blog. Thoughtfully develop your social media strategy to build a stronger brand through a network of friends, followers, and contacts. Start by posting your social media profiles on the first page of Google and try to have those sites generate enough traffic to your website or blog. Create your program so your blog updates most of your social media content automatically. Pay attention to the details when you create new content so the search engines will recognize you by your keywords. Complete your profiles, metadata, and descriptions of images using targeted keywords on each social networking site where you add content.

Creating a comprehensive Internet marketing strategy that drives quality traffic and improves your search engine results demands planning, time, and expertise. Your message and online brand are too important to leave to chance: you must consider each piece of your

Internet marketing strategy and how social media fits into the puzzle. Moreover, you must constantly monitor your brand online, control your message, and respond to criticism swiftly and skillfully. Google "social media blunders" and search YouTube for "United broke my guitar" to see what happens when you don't manage online communication effectively.

Hiring a Social Media Company

If you are considering hiring an individual or a company to handle your social media strategy, follow these four steps:

1. Visit their personal social media sites and business pages to see how many friends and followers they have.
2. Review their connections to see if they are connected with other *online influencers*.
3. Ask them what programs they have built, for which companies, and keywords they have targeted.
4. Search the companies' names. The SERPs will show you how effective the programs are.

Now that you understand the social media tools available, you can create a strategy for using them effectively. You already have your targeted keyword list, you have created your editorial calendar, and you have set up and integrated a few social sites with content from your blog. Now you can create an overall plan to determine which sites you want to add to your toolbox, what kind of internal resources and staff members you have available to manage your program, what to outsource, and how much you can budget for professional help.

Budgeting for Social Media

Social media consulting firms should understand websites, SEO, public relations, and social media, and how these elements work together. Most consultants will work on retainer for a specified number of hours monthly. The hourly rate consultants charge varies from $75–$200. You can start with a monthly budget of $1,000–$2,500 if you have internal resources to help develop content, manually publish updates, and monitor sites. The social medial companies will manage the editorial calendar, write most of the content, edit all content for SEO and SMO, help monitor the online profiles and accounts, and help you direct your internal team's efforts so they produce the desired results. If you plan to outsource social media because you have minimal staff to support it, you can expect to spend $3,000–$5,000 per month.

Internet Advertising

5

The goals of Internet and traditional advertising are similar. You buy an ad targeting the market you want to reach, hope people see it, and wait for prospects to contact you. Internet advertising is more effective than other types of ads because it speeds this process. That's why experts predict that print advertising spending will continue to decline while Internet advertising spending increases. The reason for this migration of capital is simple: consumers of all ages are spending more and more time on the Internet whereas print newspaper and magazine readership has been declining.

Moreover, in a tough market and economic environment, where companies have continually cut budgets and tried to identify better ways to advertise and spend their declining dollars, online spending in the United States continues to grow steadily. In 2006, online advertising spending was about $16.9 billion. By 2010 it was $25.8 billion, and experts expect double-digit growth for the next several years. By 2015, online advertising spending is expected to exceed $49.5 billion.[5]

An Internet advertising campaign includes *banner ads* and other links on select and targeted websites, text and image ads on search engine pages for keywords, social network advertising, online classified advertising of home listings, and other paid ads. If you are fortunate enough to have a budget for it, online advertising should supplement, rather than supplant, your organic SEO efforts. Before you pay for online advertising, consider how much quality traffic it will generate and whether it will benefit your SEO strategy.

Internet advertising results are easier to track than the results from SEO and social media campaigns. John Wanamaker, considered the father of the department store, once said, "Half the money I spend on advertising is wasted; the trouble is I don't know which half." I don't like wasting half of my clients' advertising budget, I want to be effective with their entire budget, so I track ad results.

When you purchase an ad, you want to know whether the amount of traffic generated is worth the cost. New home marketers consider the acquisition cost of leads, or how much they must spend to get one person to visit a website, one person to visit our sales center, one person to write a contract, and one person to close on a new home. Your acquisition costs will vary by market and by company type. A remodeler's acquisition costs will vary from a custom home builder's, which will vary from a production builder's. No matter what type of business you're in, you must track the acquisition cost of advertising so you know the value of each media source.

Google Analytics and other website tracking software allow you to see the origin of traffic to your website and blog and what visitors do on your sites. Beyond using the standard Google Analytics source report, you can include a unique link for each ad, website, keyword, or banner to send traffic to your website. I've already discussed landing pages. Another tool is the Google Analytics URL Builder. If you use Google Analytics as your tracking software, you can vary the code used to link each ad to your website. These code variations tell Google Analytics how to report traffic from a particular ad. To create a custom link for one of your ads, go to http://www.google.com/support/googleanalytics/bin/answer.py?answer=55578 or Google "URL Builder Tool." After you enter your web address, the advertising source (name of the website your ad will appear on), the medium (type of ad—banner, keyword purchase, etc.), and the name of your incentive, the tool will generate a link you can send to the advertiser to use as the link back to your website.

Internet Advertising Options

You can place paid advertising, like a banner with a link to your website, on other websites. It seems like almost every industry website will let you pay them to put a banner or some other kind of link back to your site on theirs. This chapter will focus on the most popular and effective types of online advertising. Besides banners, these include *pay per click (PPC)* ads, and *search engine marketing (SEM)*.

Banner ads are online versions of slick magazine advertising. They are designed to attract attention and generate clicks. You might pay a monthly fee or the cost could be related to an ad's effectiveness in generating clicks (*pay for performance*). Your cost-benefit analysis for online advertising should consider the following:

- An ad's location on the screen
- Whether you will share the location with other advertisers (various ads rotate in sequence on the user's screen) and, if so, with how many others
- How many views and clicks the ad is projected to attract

After you purchase an ad, you must track the number of quality visitors to your website it generates. Chapter 7 discusses tracking in detail.

Companies that sell Internet advertising will often focus on *impressions*, or the number of times your banner will appear on a web page where a visitor will see it. These companies sell ads based on *CPM*, or *cost per thousand* impressions. For example, you might purchase a banner for $500 that will run for a month and is expected to yield 10,000 impressions, for a cost of $50 per 1,000 impressions. The benefit of the CPM structure is that you know in advance what your cost will be. However, if you don't track the number of times a visitor clicks the ad and what they do afterward, you can't assess the ROI from the ad. If the ad generates five clicks a month with each visitor to your website viewing 3–6 pages and one visitor who comes to your sales center, the ad is worth $500. If the ad generates 400 clicks to your website but all of these visitors look at one page and then leave, the ad probably was not a worthwhile expenditure. An important part of generating traffic from an ad purchase is the ad itself. It has to be designed well, have the right message and a good call to action. Your task is to find the right combination of creative design and call to action, ad placement, and budget to drive the best traffic for the lowest acquisition cost.

Another advertising model is pay for performance, commonly referred to as pay per click (*PPC*) or *cost per click* (*CPC*). With PPC, you pay only for clicks to your website from the ad. Although you don't know your cost in advance, I like this pricing structure because you get what you pay for. As with CPM advertising, you must track the quality of traffic you get from the ad. Google AdWords is the most commonly used PPC advertising. It is one example of search engine marketing.

Search Engine Marketing

The ads that appear in the sponsored links section of a SERP are search engine marketing. Although consumers are more likely to click organic SERP links than sponsored links such as AdWords and PPC advertising, you should supplement your organic SEO efforts with a search engine marketing strategy. You can use SEM to jump-start your primary key-words as you begin an SEO program and to target secondary and ter-tiary keywords important to your SEO campaign, but not as important as the primary keywords. PPC advertising can improve your company's results for competitive primary words, but it should not replace your SEO efforts.

PPC is a viable strategy when you are confident that you can convert clicks to buyers. Establish a monthly budget for PPC and tell the search engines how much you are willing to pay for each click for each keyword. As long as your budget and bid are realistic, the search engines will display your ad in their sponsored links section just the right number of times to get the right number of clicks.

In an SEM campaign, you determine in advance the specific search terms you want to trigger your ad's appearance on the SERP. Your ad can be text only or an image-based banner. You can link all of your ads to your home page or you can develop a more sophisticated strategy to improve conversion by using a different link for each word you target (with the Google URL Builder Tool mentioned earlier in this chapter) and then tailor a landing page on your website for each ad. Building specific landing pages for keywords or ads is like making a warm call to a referral; you keep the visitor focused on why they came to your site and help convert leads to buyers.

An effective SEM program will place PPC banner ads, text links, and information about your site on prime SERP real estate (top and right side of page). Some SEO experts believe PPC encourages Google to visit your site and assess its relevance based on the words you are buying, although Google officials deny this claim. Now that you know the dif-ference between SEO and SEM, avoid companies that claim they do SEO but really do only SEM. Although buying AdWords may be a good strategy for your company, it is not an SEO strategy; it is an advertising strategy.

Some companies buy SEM words in bulk and resell them to cli-ents. They also manage SEM programs for their clients, in some cases offering research tools to help clients become more successful with their search terms. Reach Local and AdZoo are two examples. But you or your marketing or SEO company can manage your SEM program without an additional company. The option you choose depends on your resources, including your budget.

Budget

A budget for SEM ranges from $500–$1,000 and up. Spending less won't generate enough monthly traffic or clicks to be worth the money and time it takes to manage. It is not uncommon to find popular words that cost $5 per click or more, so if your budget is $500, you will only generate 100 clicks a month. A good conversion rate is between 0.5% and approximately 2%, so $500 won't generate much quality traffic. The alternatives are to increase your budget, bid on less expensive words, or both.

Online Home Listings

Because more than 90% of home buyers start their search online, you must ensure your site and listings appear on the top real estate sites. Some sites offer free listings; on others, you must pay to advertise your company and listings. Figure 5.1 shows the top 20 real estate websites.[6]

Realtor.com, Trulia, and Zillow receive your listings from the local multiple listing service (MLS). The MLS also may automatically deliver your listings free to Yahoo! Real Estate, AOL Real Estate, and other

	Rank	Website	Domain	Market Share	Mar '11	Feb '11	Jan '11
	1.	Realtor.com	www.realtor.com	6.50%	1	2	3
	2.	Yahoo! Real Estate	realestate.yahoo.com	6.10%	2	1	1
	3.	Zillow	www.zillow.com	5.52%	3	3	4
	4.	Trulia.com	www.trulia.com	4.75%	4	5	5
△	5.	AOL Real Estate	www.realestate.aol.com	2.91%	8	16	18
▽	6.	Rent.com	www.rent.com	2.41%	5	6	6
▽	7.	Homes.com	www.homes.com	2.18%	6	8	7
▽	8.	MSN Real Estate	realestate.msn.com	1.74%	7	7	9
	9.	ZipRealty	www.ziprealty.com	1.53%	9	9	8
△	10.	FrontDoor Real Estate	www.frontdoor.com	1.51%	57	4	2
▽	11.	Apartment Guide	www.apartmentguide.com	1.49%	10	10	10
	12.	MyNewPlace	www.mynewplace.com	1.19%	12	11	11
△	13.	Rentals.com	www.rentals.com	1.15%	15	12	13
▽	14.	RE/MAX Real Estate	www.remax.com	1.13%	11	14	15
△	15.	Weichert.com	www.weichert.com	1.11%	16	20	19
▽	16.	Apartments.com	www.apartments.com	1.10%	13	13	12
▽	17.	ForRent.com	www.forrent.com	1.03%	14	15	14
	18.	LoopNet	www.loopnet.com	0.94%	18	18	16
	19.	Listingbook Services	www.listingbook.com	0.92%	19	21	23
▽	20.	HomeAway	www.homeaway.com	0.87%	17	17	17

Hitwise Top 20 Real Estate Websites

The triangles next to the listings indicate a change in position from the last time the Hitwise report was run. (Reprinted with permission from Experian Hitwise)

websites. On all of these sites, you can enhance your listings with additional photos, descriptions, your company logo, and contact information.

Realtor.com

Realtor.com is the official site of the National Association of Realtors (NAR). It only displays properties listed by Realtors from the MLS. This site is branded very well by NAR for Realtor-listed properties and is the online leader with more than 6% market share of online real estate websites. If your homes are listed by a Realtor, then they will appear on Realtor.com. Your Realtor can enhance his or her listings with photos, virtual tours, descriptions, open house dates, and other information for a small monthly fee. In addition, if you are a Realtor, you can brand all of your listings with a logo and your contact information. These enhancements increase *page views* of listings compared with generic listings.

In addition to enhancing home listings, you can purchase banner ads or pay to have listings featured at the top of search results pages in a given market. The success of these approaches depends on the specific market, so monitor the ROI using your traffic report. Although Realtor.com's association with NAR lends the website credibility, the site includes only completed homes listed with members of NAR. Therefore, builders may not be able to showcase base plans unless the MLS allows you to list a to-be-built (TBB) home.

Trulia

Like Realtor.com, Trulia.com is a real estate listing website where you can claim and enhance listings. You can also buy banners on the pages that appear in your market on a CPM basis. You can budget the number of monthly impressions you want and contract for that specific number. Properties don't have to be completed homes listed on the MLS by Realtors; Trulia allows and encourages listing base plans for every community (fig. 5.2)

Although the listings can be effective, the Trulia features I have found most useful to improving your SERP and increasing your visibility are not the listings, but the social media tools the site includes. Trulia Voices is designed to connect consumers with real estate professionals (fig. 5.3). Consumers can post a question on Trulia Voices and any participating real estate professional can provide an answer. Answering consumers' questions enhances your reputation and credibility. Trulia also allows you to create and publish a blog on the site.

Trulia Listings

Trulia's listings get a large volume of traffic. Make sure your homes are there.
(Reprinted with permission from Trulia.com)

FIGURE 5.2

FIGURE 5.3

Trulia Voices

Trulia Voices is a great social media tool and third-party blog on a site with high traffic.
(Reprinted with permission from Trulia.com)

Zillow

Zillow is another popular real estate listing site. It has 5.5% market share of online real estate traffic, which equates to 25.1 million monthly visitors.[7] Zillow not only displays your homes on a map, but shows valuation data for each listing. The valuations ("Zestimates") that Zillow displays consider all recently sold properties, even foreclosed homes and short sales. Consumers really like this map and features from Zillow, but it certainly presents some challenges for builders selling TBB and new homes near distressed properties. Whether you advertise on Zillow or not, if the valuation displayed on your listing is lower than your asking price, be prepared to educate buyers about the true value when they walk in the door to your sales center and are ready to negotiate. Another less significant challenge with Zillow is that your communities may not be on the map if they are still under development and construction, which can confuse potential buyers. Because Zillow attracts so much traffic, however, you should try to incorporate the site in your strategy, especially if home prices are stable in your area. Figure 5.4 shows a Zillow listing page with the Zestimates on the map at the top.

Apartments.com and Apartment Guide

Multifamily developers and builders can list their properties on Apartments.com and ApartmentGuide.com. These sites operate their paid listings and banner advertising similarly to Realtor.com and Trulia. Consumers can view photos, floor plans, and products; check availability; and contact the community. With as much traffic as they drive, a multi-family developer should look at these two.

Other Niche and Industry Sites

In addition to the aforementioned sites, there are many others where you can post information about your inventory homes and the communities in which you build. TheBDX.com (a merger of MOVE.com and NewHomeSource.com), focuses specifically on the new home industry, rather than generic real estate. You can list your communities, base plans, and inventory homes. The cost for listing your homes on the BDX network of sites is based on how many communities you list, rather than the number of homes or listings you submit. After you purchase the base product by placing your communities and homes on the BDX, you can pay an additional fee for banner advertising.

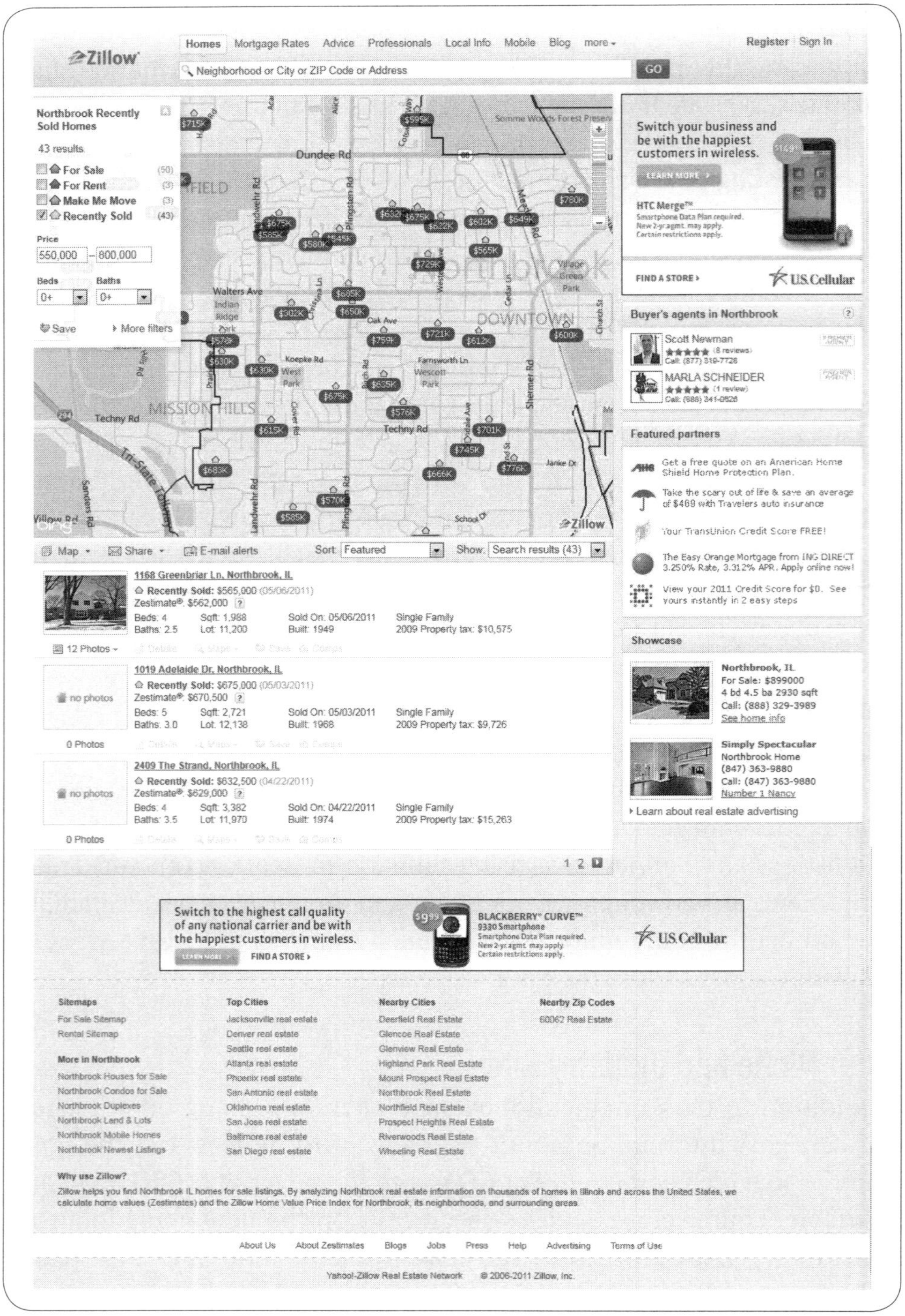

FIGURE 5.4

Zillow Listings

Consumers like the Zestimates on Zillow. (Reprinted with permission from Zillow, Inc.)

New Homes Directory is another new home industry website where you can list your homes and communities. As with Google AdWords and the PPC model, charges kick in when a visitor clicks a listing and visits your website. However, the fees are capped per community. New Homes Directory stops billing you for clicks when you reach your maximum budget, but unlike Google, your ad will continue to appear and generate traffic.

Like Trulia, New Homes Directory includes social media and PR opportunities. You can get stories and content published, with links back to your site. Carol Flammer, author of *Social Media for Home Builders 2.0: It's Easier Than You Think*, and Carol Ruiz of red rocket LA Marketing and PR, collaborate to provide helpful industry information based on questions that builders submit (fig. 5.5).

"Free" websites

A number of websites will list your homes for free, but you must invest time to enter your listings and update the information. Evaluate the ROI on free sites: consider how much time you spend entering and updating the website compared with the amount of qualified traffic you get. Even if you don't pay a fee to list homes, if the listings garner no quality traffic, eliminate the site from your Internet marketing toolbox. The Resources at the back of the book include both listing sites and tools.

Craigslist

Craigslist is an online classified marketplace. Unlike on the other sites, a simple ad with a couple of pictures and a few links with anchor text gets a better response on Craigslist than a full-color "slick" e-flyer. I'm not sure why this is the case. Perhaps consumers are accustomed to the classified text prevalent on Craigslist and they like it that way. Or

Own Your Listings

If you list available homes on your website, you should store them in a database that will feed them to other sites where you want to list them. Depending on the MLS's IDX data feed is generally not a good option for your website or the Internet listing sites for three reasons. First, the MLS's data feed generally takes several days to update and feed the listing sites, so the data can be old and outdated. Second, the MLS uses Realtor jargon and abbreviations that brokers may understand, but consumers may not. Third, the MLS controls and owns the listings they feed.

You should own your content and data. After all, the home listings are yours. Most of the listing sites allow you to submit your listings electronically, so they don't have to be manually updated daily. But the data transfer process is complex and can be different for each website. You should format your listings in *Extensible Markup Language (XML)* to transfer them from your database to all Internet listing sites that will display them.

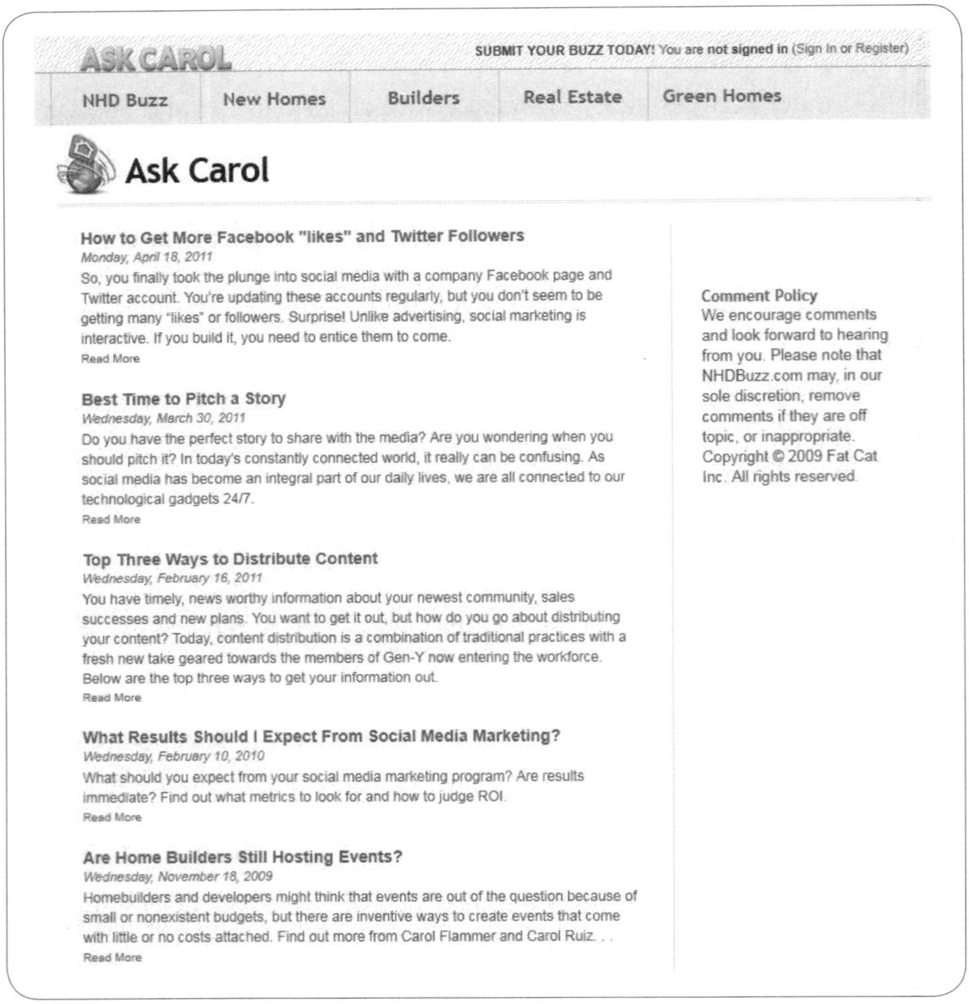

SUBMIT YOUR BUZZ TODAY! You are **not signed in** (Sign In or Register)

ASK CAROL

| NHD Buzz | New Homes | Builders | Real Estate | Green Homes |

Ask Carol

How to Get More Facebook "likes" and Twitter Followers
Monday, April 18, 2011
So, you finally took the plunge into social media with a company Facebook page and Twitter account. You're updating these accounts regularly, but you don't seem to be getting many "likes" or followers. Surprise! Unlike advertising, social marketing is interactive. If you build it, you need to entice them to come.
Read More

Best Time to Pitch a Story
Wednesday, March 30, 2011
Do you have the perfect story to share with the media? Are you wondering when you should pitch it? In today's constantly connected world, it really can be confusing. As social media has become an integral part of our daily lives, we are all connected to our technological gadgets 24/7.
Read More

Top Three Ways to Distribute Content
Wednesday, February 16, 2011
You have timely, news worthy information about your newest community, sales successes and new plans. You want to get it out, but how do you go about distributing your content? Today, content distribution is a combination of traditional practices with a fresh new take geared towards the members of Gen-Y now entering the workforce. Below are the top three ways to get your information out.
Read More

What Results Should I Expect From Social Media Marketing?
Wednesday, February 10, 2010
What should you expect from your social media marketing program? Are results immediate? Find out what metrics to look for and how to judge ROI.
Read More

Are Home Builders Still Hosting Events?
Wednesday, November 18, 2009
Homebuilders and developers might think that events are out of the question because of small or nonexistent budgets, but there are inventive ways to create events that come with little or no costs attached. Find out more from Carol Flammer and Carol Ruiz . . .
Read More

Comment Policy
We encourage comments and look forward to hearing from you. Please note that NHDBuzz.com may, in our sole discretion, remove comments if they are off topic, or inappropriate. Copyright © 2009 Fat Cat Inc. All rights reserved.

FIGURE 5.5   NHDBuzz Ask Carol
Industry niche sites will drive traffic to your homes, and provide places to syndicate your content. (Reprinted with permission from Fat Cat Inc., Murrieta, California)

maybe they go to Craigslist to do business with people rather than companies and they see a flyer as too Madison Avenue. Regardless of the reason, minimal graphics on this no-frills site make it easy to use it to drive traffic to your website. Don't take my word for it, do your own A/B testing of ad alternatives on Craigslist.

Designate a person to post listings daily or weekly, depending on your resources, to make the most of the site. Listings automatically expire after seven days. Don't duplicate them. This violates Craigslist policy and the site can remove your ads. Craigslist can become one of your top five sources of referrals, so you should include it in your marketing strategy.

Next Steps

Now that you have an idea of the advertising sites and the types of ads you can run, it is time to create a full marketing and advertising budget. Review the marketing budget calculations at the end of chapter 2 to determine what your total budget should be. Identify all of your fixed marketing expenses and define how much you need for your Internet budget. Subtract the cost of building or updating your new website. The remaining amount is your SEO, SEM, blogging and advertising budget. Keep this number handy. When you learn in chapter 7 how to analyze your traffic and determine your return on investment, you will be ready to start evaluating how to spend this budget effectively.

Leads and Conversion Marketing   6

Once you have an attractive, well-designed, and search-engine friendly website; an effective social media program that syndicates your message and builds your brand; an organic SEO strategy to feed spider bait to the search engines; and you are running online ads, how do you handle the influx of leads?

Sales and marketing professionals define leads in a variety of ways, especially when they are coming from different sources. I consider everyone who may be interested in buying your product a lead, whether they completed your online form, picked up the phone to call you, drove to your community, or clicked a link on your website for more information. How or whether you move forward with each lead is your choice.

Understanding Leads

When buyers call or enter your model center, your sales team should assume they have been to your website and should consider them be-back visitors even if they are walking in the door for the first time. Your sales associates should ask their sales center visitors what they thought of your website and whether they found what they were looking for on it. Remind your sales team often that most prospects, your buyers and the visitors to your sales center have already been on your website looking at the information that appeals to them. This should establish the buyer as a repeat visitor to your sales team. Your sales team will be more effective at closing these buyers if they assume the walk-ins and calls have done their homework about your homes and communities and are interested in your product. If you have a salesperson who continues to tell you that their buyers are not online and they are the less than 10%, it may be time to hire a new sales agent.

Lead Follow-Up (or Lack of It)

Most leads (in this case, I am referring to e-mail lead requests from a builder's website) go unanswered. I know this because my company conducts online mystery shopping (sometimes for prospective clients and sometimes just for fun). We complete the contact form on a builder's website and then wait for a response. We use a Gmail, Hotmail, or yahoo e-mail account with a fictitious name because sometimes the sales representatives know us. The response we get is abysmal. Most companies never reply to our requests. If we are lucky, we get an automated response when we fill out the form and one personal response from an agent one time. Don't be one of these builders. Website visitors who use their precious time to fill out your form, give you their e-mail addresses or contact information, and ask you a question are hot buyers. "You cannot follow up too quickly with these leads, only too slowly!" says leading online sales trainer Meredith Oliver.

The best way to ensure your sales team knows what to do, does what you expect, and follows up on leads is to use a customer relationship management (CRM) or lead management system. You can purchase off-the-shelf CRM systems with various features, some quite complex. Following is a concise overview of the features to look for:

Integration with your website. Many systems can exchange data reciprocally with your website. That is, they can both automatically add leads from the website to the CRM system and deliver key current listing and inventory data to the website. Having the information the users type in your online form automatically populate your CRM system is a real time saver. Likewise, the web-page-listing-to-CRM feature makes duplicate typing a thing of the past.

Reminders for your sales representatives. Once your leads are in, some CRM systems will automatically remind your sales agents to call, e-mail, or otherwise follow up with them on a set schedule. Tracking that follow up with notes in the system so you can tell what kind of interaction your sales team has with a potential buyer will help throughout the sales process.

E-mail correspondence. Most CRM systems have built-in e-mail marketing. Find out if they can send attractive e-mail flyers in HTML with graphics, and if you can set up automated e-mail campaigns for follow-up. For example, when a lead is added, the system should send an automated but personalized e-mail message with the sales agent's contact information.

If the lead has not responded to your agent after three days or seven days, you can schedule additional e-mail messages, weekly if necessary, for up to a few weeks.

Opt out. With the *CAN-SPAM Act* and other legal issues related to e-mail marketing, look for systems that can help you manage your opt-out list (people who do not want you to continue contacting them).

E-mail Marketing. This is different from sending e-mail correspondence to individual leads. Some CRM systems can send bulk e-mail messages to all your contacts, or to a sub-list of contacts. You might want to use this function to e-mail a monthly newsletter or a one-time marketing flyer to all of your prospects announcing a new special or incentive. You can supplement this feature with e-mail marketing software as an alternative, if your CRM system otherwise does what you need but does not handle e-mail marketing well.

Building Your E-mail Marketing List

Your website, CRM system, and e-mail marketing program work together to help you build a list of quality e-mail addresses of people who have contacted you for more information. Don't worry if your selected CRM system is not able to send out bulk e-mail marketing pieces. Several good software programs are listed in the Resources section in the back of the book that can supplement your e-mail marketing. The best and safest way to get a list of accurate, usable e-mail addresses is to have visitors fill out the form on your website to join your e-mail list. Here are five other ways to build lists:

1. **Capture e-mail addresses** from your website and blog through a contact form or registration page for an incentive or promotion.
2. **Create a form on your Facebook page** that links to your blog or website. Facebook continually changes the advanced functionality on your business page tabs or links so use the preferred method. Today, we use Facebook Markup Language (FBML) boxes and HTML iFrames. These are two good tools for capturing e-mail addresses, but they both require technical programming.
3. **Create a list of Realtors** who have shown one of your properties in the past 12–24 months from your existing registration cards.

4. **Collect business cards at networking events,** such as local HBA meetings, Realtor association meetings, and consumer shows.

5. **Train your on-site sales people to gather e-mail addresses** and other contact information from prospects.

There are many other ways to create e-mail contact lists; however, you will get the best marketing results and minimize the risk of becoming a spammer or being blacklisted on search engines if you build lists from people who currently have a relationship with you or your company, have done business with you in the past, or have contacted you for more information. Although building lists using this approach takes time and effort, you will get higher quality contacts and be more likely to convert them to buyers.

The CAN-SPAM Act

The CAN-SPAM Act applies to all commercial e-mail messages, which the law defines as "any electronic mail message the primary purpose of which is the commercial advertisement or promotion of a commercial product or service." This includes e-mail that promotes content on commercial websites. Contrary to popular belief, the act doesn't apply only to bulk e-mail and the law makes no exception for business-to-business e-mail or messages to former customers. You should know the law and consult your attorney about laws regarding commercial e-mail, and monitor what others are doing on your behalf. You are liable for your e-mail messages even if you have hired another company or person to send your e-mail. Following are some legal requirements:

- Your "To," "From" or "Reply" lines must clearly identify the person or business sending the e-mail message.
- The "Subject" line must accurately represent the message content.
- If your message is an ad, you must clearly disclose this. The law doesn't specify where or how.
- Your e-mail must include your valid physical postal address. You can use your office address or a post office box, or a mailbox at another location may fulfill this requirement.
- Recipients must have a way to opt out of receiving future e-mail from you. This could be through an opt-out link in your message

or instructions for the recipient to reply to the e-mail or visit a website.

■ You must honor opt-out requests promptly. The method you choose for opting out must be available for at least 30 days after the date you sent the e-mail message and you must be able to process an opt-out request within 10 days of receiving it.

Although e-mail marketing is an effective way to communicate with prospects, privacy laws and laws to reduce unwanted e-mail impact the use and effectiveness of e-mail marketing. Collecting e-mail addresses from your website and sales center visitors has always been the best way to generate a list. After you have a list, you can send regular e-flyers or a monthly newsletter to update your leads and prospects about your company, homes, and communities, and to keep your name in front of them. Use e-mail to supplement regular personal communication with Realtors as well.

E-mail marketing is challenging, legally and technically. If you approach it clumsily you will do more harm than good to your marketing efforts. If you send the wrong kind of e-mail or send messages to the wrong person or list, your e-mail domain can be banned from sending e-mail— even to regular clients. Moreover, your company could disappear from search engine results. You may not be able to reverse these consequences.

If an e-mail program that monitors and filters messages for users identifies an e-mail marketer or e-mail message as spam, no message from that source will get through—not even personal communication. You can check http://www.mxtoolbox.com/blacklist.aspx to see if your domain is on it (fig. 6.1). Enter your domain, (e.g., mrelevance.com) and click MX Lookup. When the site returns your domain's IP address, click Blacklist Check (fig. 6.2). If any spam list on the results page returns an error or message next to it, you must contact the list owner to have your domain removed from their spam list. Company policies for honoring requests for removal vary. Even if you convince a company to remove you from a spam list, the process can take two to three weeks. The best strategy is to avoid being labeled a spammer to begin with.

If the search engines tag your domain or IP address as spam or a location with inappropriate content, they may remove your entire domain from the search results index. In other words, even if someone types your company name into Google, your site will not appear. Four common causes of search engine blacklisting are (1) Comments on your blog were published without being moderated. (2) Your website or blog is

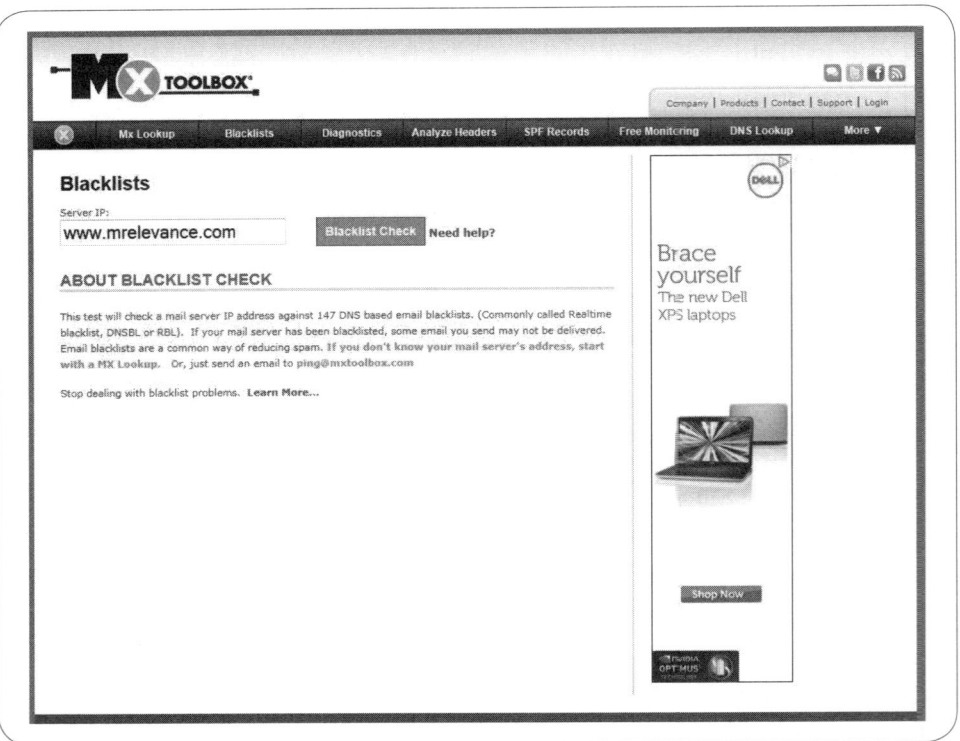

in a shared hosting environment where there is another site that has been tagged for spam or inappropriate content. (3) You have sent bulk e-mail to a list that violates the CAN-SPAM act. (4) A recipient reported your e-mail to an e-mail service as spam. Avoid all of these situations. Beyond the public relations and marketing headaches, your company could suffer legal consequences under the CAN-SPAM Act.[8] Know and follow the law, and use caution when blasting e-mail.

I approach all my clients' e-mail lists with caution and suspicion because builders and Realtors sometimes compile lists from the local MLS or purchase them from other sources. If you follow either of these practices, or are considering them, consult with your local MLS and your attorney first. If you proceed, you will need a plan to clean the list to avoid being tagged as a spammer. The best solution is to compile your list manually using only the information gathered from people who contacted you first. I do not endorse or recommend obtaining a list any other way. Even if you apply each list-cleaning guideline that follows, you still could be

FIGURE 6.2 **MxToolbox Blacklist Search**
Notice how many potential spam lists could blacklist your domain. (Reprinted with permission from MxToolBox Inc.)

targeted as a spammer. Therefore, I recommend paying an e-mail marketing company to send to their list instead of purchasing or exchanging lists.

Cleaning Your List

Cleaning your purchased or borrowed e-mail lists is long and tedious. If you choose this method, follow these eight steps:

1. Remove all AOL and Bellsouth e-mail addresses. These two companies have a low threshold for spam. Often your domain will be added to their blacklist with as few as 5 or 6 complaints.
2. Separate lists with more than 750 e-mail addresses into smaller lists of no more than 500–750. (Most marketing companies don't allow you to upload, at least initially, lists larger than this.)

3. Upload your lists several days or weeks apart. This minimizes the chance that the company you are uploading the list to will watch your account because they see a list growing quickly.

4. Create an e-flyer with an offer or an incentive that asks recipients to subscribe to your e-mail list to receive the offer. It must be creative and captivating.

5. Create an online form website visitors can use to subscribe to your e-mail list.

6. Create a Thank You page linked to the form and an automatic response that e-mails subscribers to your e-mail list. Both the Thank You page and the auto-response should contain your company name.

7. Send out the first e-flyer to each sub-list, and to no more than 750 addresses or so each day. You don't want hundreds of people simultaneously to report your e-mail as spam. It will take two to three weeks to contact a list of 10,000 names.

8. Remove all *bounced e-mail* and opt-out e-mail addresses from your lists.

After you have sent one e-mail message to each address on the list, rinse and repeat. This time, combine some of your smaller lists into lists of 1,000–1,500 names and send to one list each day. You don't want more names on the second list because you must still avoid your e-mail generating complaints and bounced e-mail addresses. You may need to e-mail 3–4 flyers before opt-outs stop or, conversely, a recipient reports the e-mail as spam, so you want to spread your communication over several weeks. Tweak each message to maintain urgency but focus on persuading recipients to opt in by subscribing to your mailing list. Repeat these processes until you are able to combine all of the lists into a single list of people you have e-mailed about 4 times in 6–8 weeks. You should send a final e-mail, when you have finished the process, to reintroduce your company and tell recipients how to opt out of your e-mail.

At the end of this process, you will have two lists: one list of people who completed the form and registered for your incentive and a second list of possibly valid e-mail addresses that did not take any action. You can add the first list, but not the second, to your existing contacts and manually collected e-mail addresses. Both lists should be clean and safe to send to.

Outsourcing E-flyers

You can outsource the task of sending e-flyers instead of buying and cleaning up an e-mail address list. Considering the time and resources required to compile and clean lists, this option is well worth paying for. Most companies that have compiled their own lists slowly over time and can send your e-flyer charge $150–$500 per e-flyer. The fee is for sending the message and maintaining the e-mail lists. You probably will need to write the copy and provide the design for your message. Also, if you choose to outsource, you should still budget time for tracking the amount of traffic each e-flyer sends to your website. This will help you improve your messages and design.

Scheduling E-flyers

After you have a clean list, create a schedule for your e-mail marketing. One e-blast per month is plenty. You can easily create monthly newsletters from your blog content. This creative repurposing saves time, maintains a consistent message, and reinforces your targeted keywords for SEO. Choose three to four popular blog posts from the past month, write an enticing teaser for each, and include a link to the complete blog entry. You can supplement this content with advertisements to highlight special offers, incentives, or events (figs. 6.3–6.6). Encourage readers to print these ads and bring them when they visit your homes and communities. Strive to generate clicks.

Making Change Happen

As a former on-site sales associate and a consultant who helped a few top 10 builders select their CRM systems, I know there are many factors to consider. Get your sales team involved in the selection process as early as pos-

Mystery Shop

It can be fun, or frustrating, to find out how well your sales team follows up with leads from your website. If your sales are not as robust as you would like, it may be because your contact form is broken or your sales team does not reply to web inquiries as they should. Do not tell your sales team you are shopping your company and competitors. That's why the exercise is called a "mystery" shop.

1. Create a Gmail account using a fictitious name.
2. Complete the form on your website using this new e-mail account and name.
3. Go to your top 5 competitors' websites and fill out their forms with the new e-mail address as well.
4. Monitor your new e-mail box for 90 days and document what each company sends you.
5. Create a lead management and e-mail marketing strategy for your company that builds on the best communication you receive.

 A Clear Call to Action
Notice the clear call to action, "Click Here to become a fan of Highland Homes on Facebook!" (Reprinted with permission from Highland Homes, Lakeland, Florida)

sible. This helps garner their buy in, which makes implementation and training easier.

Your sales team is the best source of information about lead follow-up. Associates can tell you what they are doing at each point in the process and how often. Brainstorming with them about specific ways to improve the process or their wish list for lead management can point you toward the right technology solutions. Write everything down in your brainstorming session(s) and share the results with your entire team so everyone understands what lead follow-up means to your company. Don't forget to mystery shop your company every 90–120 days to make sure your vision of lead follow-up materializes.

FIGURE 6.4 **Offering Incentives**

You can offer a meaningful incentive to attract buyers to a Grand Opening event. (Reprinted with permission from Highland Homes, Lakeland, Florida)

FIGURE 6.5 Creating Urgency

Create urgency with your messages. (Source: Reprinted with permission from Highland Homes, Lakeland, Florida)

Limited Time Offer

Limited-time offers like these create urgency. (Reprinted with permission from Highland Homes, Lakeland, FL)

Measuring Results and Determining Success

7

Throughout this book I have talked about goals and results. If you follow my instructions and complete all the exercises, you will have built a solid Internet marketing program that is integrated with your social media, public relations, advertising, and communication strategy. The only way to know whether it's working, though, is to track KPIs discussed previously. This chapter will help you understand how to measure the effectiveness of each part of your program so you can make data-driven decisions to improve results.

After you integrate the components of your Internet marketing program into your business strategy, you must constantly evaluate whether Internet marketing is helping you achieve your goals and driving traffic to your sales centers. Contracts and sales are the main goal of any marketing program, but achieving intermediate milestones for each piece of your Internet marketing program will help you reach the ultimate goal. These milestones include

- increasing quality website traffic and converting more online traffic into sales center visits by providing the information home buyers are looking for;
- improving SERP rankings for the specific keywords your SEO program is targeting and filling up the search engine results pages with your primary content;
- increasing the size and reach of your social media sites by boosting the number of friends, fans, and followers in your network and interacting with influencers;
- increasing the open and click-through rates of your e-mail marketing newsletters and flyers; and
- prompting your website visitors to drive to your sales center to see your models, call your sales agents, or complete your online contact form so you capture their e-mail addresses.

To continuously improve your online marketing and achieve these goals, you must track and analyze your website visitors' behavior and their social media sphere of influence. Tracking and understanding this information is critical to your Internet marketing strategy. Analyzing the trends of web visitor behavior, interaction, and other metrics over time allows you to assess your website, social media, public relations, e-mail marketing, and advertising program effectiveness. You will also be able to calculate ROI for each line item in your marketing budget using your website *tracking report*. First, though, you must understand the appropriate goals for each Internet marketing component and where to look for these results.

Website Tracking Software

To monitor the details regarding *visits* to your website, blog, or both, install tracking software on every page of your website and your blog. This entails embedding code in each page. Some tracking software packages, like Google Analytics and AWStats, are free. Others, like Omniture, incur setup and monthly monitoring costs. I use Google Analytics because it is free and easy to use. You merely copy and paste code on each page of your website or in a file (like a *footer file*) already included on each page of your website, and Google Analytics does the rest. Tracking your website will tell you everything you need to know about your marketing program, what is working, and what needs to be changed.

AWStats and Webalizer are software packages that are set up on your hosting company's server and give you a high-level overview of some of your KPIs, but not full detail of any of them. One distinguishing feature of Google Analytics compared with tracking programs hosted on your server (such as AWStats) is its ability to filter results by time period. You can select a date range for evaluating traffic and compare trends over time such as month to month or year to year. No matter which software package you choose, check the KPIs at least monthly and adjust your strategy accordingly.

Setting Up Google Analytics

1. Create an account in Google or log in to your existing Google account.
2. Go to analytics.google.com (you may need to log in again).
3. Create a website profile by following the instructions on the screen and clicking through the Help wizard.
4. The last page of the wizard contains the tracking code to use on your website or blog.
5. Highlight all of the code and copy it.
6. Paste the code into the footer file of your website or blog.

Google Analytics and paid solutions like Omniture enable data filtering, reporting of KPIs, and *granular reporting*. They allow you to analyze your website's effectiveness in holding visitors' attention and capturing enough information to create a lead for your sales team to follow up. After you install the necessary code on your site, you can begin measuring results so you can use the data to modify your marketing program to ensure success.

Assessing Traffic Quantity and Quality

Track the amount of quality website traffic. It can and should lead to more sales center traffic. Three important indicators of quality website traffic are visits, *absolute unique visitors*, and page views. These numbers measure overall traffic to your website or blog. A visit (or *session*), according to Google, is "a period of interaction between a browser and a website." For example, when you first arrive on a website and begin to browse, that is a visit. If you leave the website but return later to look at something different, the subsequent visit counts as a second visit, but you are still only one visitor. (If you don't click on anything for more than 30 minutes on the first visit, it counts as two visits.) In order to achieve your goals, you need to monitor your traffic and the statistics about each session.

To understand what the numbers mean, consider the following example: you go to my blog (http://www.MitchLevinson.com), read the first post in the stream on the home page, and then click to the About page to read more about me. You then leave my site by clicking the link to one of my client's sites. Your visit to my website is considered one visit, one absolute unique visitor, and two page views. If you came back to my site a few hours later and visited the home page, commented on the post you had read earlier and went to the contact page to ask me a question, Google Analytics would now count two visits, one absolute unique visitor, and five page views. The system distinguishes between a new visitor and a returning visitor using a *cookie* it installs on your computer when you visit my site the first time. Attracting more people to your site more often and to view more pages will improve your results.

Of course, as previously discussed, just getting more traffic is not always better. What you really want is quality traffic from buyers who are looking for information about your products. Just as you qualify leads in your sales process, you should assess the quality of traffic to your websites. *Pages per visit* and *average time on site* are two indicators of the quality of your website traffic. In general, you can assume the longer a visitor stays on your site and the more pages they view, the more interested they are in your product and the more likely it is that they will visit your sales center or contact you. The amount of time users spend on your website and how many pages they view per visit tells you whether your site quickly provided users with the information they were looking for and whether they stayed on the site and looked for more. Each site will have its own benchmarks and an acceptable range for these indicators. I like to see visitors spending more than 2½ minutes and viewing more than three pages. But because some sites and web pages are created to simply capture the lead and take the visitor elsewhere they may have a lower benchmark for time spent and pages viewed. On your blog that is separate from your website or a page that is designed to capture contact information on the landing page, your *bounce rate* should be higher. The bounce rate is the percentage of visitors that come to a site and look at one and only one page before they leave. Blogs, for example, have a higher bounce rate by virtue of their design. When you build them correctly with well-written content, they will spark reader interest in and draw them to other sites (such as your company website). If a goal of your blog is to be among the top five sources driving traffic to your website, your blog should capture traffic and send it to your website quickly, and therefore have a high bounce rate.

The Google Analytics' All Traffic Report shows *traffic sources.* This report shows which sources send the most and highest quality traffic to your site and provides information you can use to calculate the ROI for each Internet advertising and marketing source. Wherever you spend money or time to advertise should appear in this report so you can calculate the amount of traffic per dollar or amount of time spent. Any paid ad, your PPC program, and your SEO should drive traffic to your site. Once you know how much traffic, you can calculate your cost or effort per click.

When you know which sources drive the most traffic for the least amount of money and time, you can make wise budget choices. But that is not enough. You also need to look at the quality of the traffic from each source. Remember to look at how many pages per visit and how long visitors stayed on your website from each of those sources.

Types of Website Traffic

Your website attracts three types of traffic: search engine, referring site, and direct.

Search engine traffic includes both traffic from your SEO efforts and SEM traffic from your PPC campaigns. Google Analytics separates each traffic type as a line item so you can drill down into your results.

Referring site traffic comes to the site from inbound links on other websites or blogs. Your blog posts, online articles, online advertising, and press releases on PR sites are in this category.

Reinforcing Messages Online and Off

Convert web visitors from your offline advertising into warm leads willing to give you their contact information by building a landing page with a clever URL and a keyword-rich title on your website or blog.

Direct traffic comes from visitors typing your domain into the address bar of their web browser or selecting it from a bookmark or favorite that they have previously saved. Direct traffic trends and fluctuations should correlate with your offline marketing and branding efforts. In other words, an effective newspaper ad or other traditional advertising technique should generate a spike or increase in direct traffic visits to your website as well as traffic to your sales center.

When you run an effective SEO and social media program without much traditional media, most of your traffic will probably come from search engines and referring sources. As you make changes in social media or your SEO, you should see corresponding changes in the traffic from those sources. If you increase your online advertising budget or send out an e-flyer, you should see an increase in your referring site traffic. When you place a local newspaper ad, you should see an increase in direct traffic.

Annual Comparison and Monthly Trending

The reports mentioned so far are snapshots of your traffic. Whether the report is for a particular day, a month, or even a year, you are still viewing just a moment in time. Therefore, you must also view your KPIs, track all of the indicators discussed on a monthly basis, and examine trends over a longer time period. When you look at your traffic month over month and year over year, you will be able to see trends that coincide with movement in the housing market, the overall economy, and traditional home buying seasons. For example, you may see a pattern of increased traffic from early spring through late fall and a decline at the end of the year. Trends help you manage your expectations for

How Do You Measure Up?

Some websites that allow you to compare your site and traffic with other websites'. Alexa.com, Quantcast.com, and Compete.com are three places I go to evaluate the results of client sites I manage, compared with their competitors' sites. Go to each of these sites and search your websites and blogs, and then look for your competitors.

traffic during specific periods and predict when to ramp up marketing.

Moreover, observing traffic over a multiyear period helps you allocate the marketing budget. Look at what your budget was, how much website traffic you got, how much of it led to sales center visits, and how many visits converted to sales. As with any marketing initiative, when you budget for Internet marketing using multiple months and measurements, you will get better results than if you consider only one month or one indicator. In a slow market, stability or even slight increases in traffic from one year to the next may indicate that although traffic and sales are down, you are in a better position to capture market share from your less effective competitors.

Focus on your goals and evaluate traffic regularly. The information you gather will help you understand whether your website is meeting your goals and, if not, how to modify it to make it work better. Your KPIs depend on your specific goals.

Lead Capture and Contacts

Beyond numbers of visitors, pages viewed, and where your site ranks in the search engines, you need to monitor your website's effectiveness in persuading visitors to go to your sales center, call your sales agents, or complete your online contact form with an e-mail address. You can analyze how users interact with critical pages, such as your contact form, to try to improve these results.

For example, if your contact form attracts significant traffic but doesn't generate many leads, consider whether you need to simplify it or provide an incentive for completing it. If you have a high bounce rate on the home page or the number of pages per visit is high but the time spent on your site is low, your navigation may be confusing; visitors may click around, but they get frustrated and leave the site. After you make changes to correct these problems, monitor the quantity and quality of your website traffic to see if the modifications improved results.

Monitoring Search Engine Rankings

Monitoring your site's ranking in the search engines for your targeted keywords is easy: simply go to Google or the other search engines, make sure you are not logged into your profile or account, and type in your keywords. Make sure you are logged out of your Google account because the search engine algorithms customize your search results based on your prior search history and your location. Your results list will display sites according to sites you have visited in the past. Therefore, your site's ranking will appear artificially high because you probably visit your site more often than you visit competitors' sites. If you are logged out, you will see a message to "sign in" at the upper right corner of the screen. If you are logged in, the upper right area will show your profile name.

I also use an SEO search tool, RankChecker by SEOBook. It allows you to type the URL of the website you want to track results for, add the keywords you are targeting, run the program, and see the ranking of your site for each of the words on Google, Yahoo!, and Bing. Track these results weekly or month over month. Again, you want to see improved results over time.

Check Your Rankings

1. Create your targeted keyword list.
2. Open a web browser and go to Google.
3. Make sure you are logged out of your Google account.
4. Type the first keyword in the search field.
5. Look for your sites in the first three to five pages of search results and note their rank number.
6. Repeat the process for your other primary keywords.
7. If you do not have Firefox on your computer, go to http://www.firefox.com and download and install the most current free version of the web browser.
8. Open Firefox and go to http://tools.seobook.com/firefox/rank-checker and download and install the most current free version of RankChecker by SEOBook.
9. Run the RankChecker Report for your website URL and for your primary keywords.
10. Save the report and run a similar one a week later to compare your rankings in the top search engines.

Measuring Your Social Media Reach

Measuring your social media reach and your influence online is less straightforward than checking your rankings. You must evaluate your online reputation and the sentiment for your brand, as well as how familiar people are with your name. Comments, tweets, retweets, interaction, and engagement are just a few indicators. Tracking these metrics is relatively new for social media. Because I have limited experience with the tools for monitoring these interactions, you should take the time to review the ones listed in the Resources at the back of the book and Google "social media monitoring tools" to find the right tool for you.

Measure Your "Klout"

Klout.com measures several social media metrics to calculate your Klout score and your relative reach in your online sphere of influence. Go to Klout.com and type in your Twitter handle, create an account, and associate your Facebook and LinkedIn profile with it. Klout will then calculate your Klout score, your online reach (or influence), and your amplification factor (the strength of your sphere to retweet).

Tying It All Together

Your Internet marketing strategy should connect all of your online and offline activity into a holistic program that will help you sell more homes. I hope this book will help you think through your entire strategy as well as the individual components of your Internet marketing program. You will experience positive results when you consider each component of your plan, add new elements, and build upon existing features.

For example, you should link to your blog, Facebook page, Twitter account and all other online profiles from your website, just as your Facebook page should link to your website and the other sites where you have a profile or where you are active. When you send e-mail, your e-mail signature should link to your website, blog, and Facebook page. In addition, whenever you write content, titles, profile descriptions, or any other online text, you should use keywords appropriately to feed the search engines. Following are three examples of companies that set goals for and went on to build effective and integrated Internet marketing programs.

Clearing Up Brand Confusion

Highland Homes in Lakeland, Florida (fig. 8.1), faced a similar challenge to many private builders: name recognition (or more precisely, name competition). Highland Homes is popular company name. In fact, a different Highland Homes, in Texas, owns the domain HighlandHomes.com. (The Florida company is http://www.highlandhomes.org.)

I worked with Kathie McDaniel, MIRM, vice president of sales and marketing for the Florida company, to help solidify the company's online presence. The company was selling approximately 35 homes per month when we started working together in 2007, as Florida home sales were declining along with the nationwide housing market. We started

FIGURE 8.1   **Highland Homes Home Page**
Sales almost doubled as Highland Homes increased SEO and social media even though the company cut the marketing budget by 75%. (Reprinted with permission from Highland Homes, Lakeland, Florida)

by searching Google for the company's primary keywords. The only keyword search that returned a link to the company site within the first three pages was its name. Even though the company had a budget and was spending money on advertising and marketing, it was not present on social media sites. Its website was built in *JSP*, but it was not search-engine friendly, scalable, or even stable in the hosting environment so that it would always be available.

mRELEVANCE took over management of the website late in 2007, moved it to a more stable hosting environment and began modifying it to improve performance. The site was attracting 4,000–5,000 visits when the company was forced to halve its marketing budget because of the weak housing market.

With the Highland team, mRELEVANCE recommended cutting advertising that was not earning ROI in website or sales center traffic, rebuilding the website in PHP, building a blog, and starting a social media program. Highland Homes cut the advertising budget by a full 50%. This was the strategy through 2009 and most of 2010. Website traffic grew to 6,500–7,200 visits to the website. More importantly, monthly home sales increased from 35 to 60 in less than 18 months in a down market.

In late 2010, the sales and marketing budget took another 50% cut. Even though the budget is significantly less (75%) than what it was during the housing boom, Highland Homes still maintains an average of 50 sales per month. The traffic to its website has been as high as 9,300 visitors per month and averages almost 8,000 visits per month. Moreover, Highland attributes 22% of its sales solely to its Internet marketing and social media program.

Rethinking Communication

A year after the Home Builders Association (HBA) of Greater Springfield (http://www.springfieldhba.com) revamped its website (fig. 8.2) in late 2010, average daily traffic had more than doubled and the amount of time users spent on site tripled. Activity and connections with the HBA's social networks also have increased. The website was designed, among other things, to be easily updated. SpringfieldHBA.com represents "everything we are, everything we do, in real time online," says HBA Chief Executive Officer Matt Morrow.

The Springfield HBA comprises more than 400 builders, remodelers, construction suppliers, subcontractors, and advocates for construction professionals in 10 counties in southwest Missouri. A decade ago, the association's online presence consisted of a static HBA website with a few pages of basic information that was rarely updated. The association's Internet marketing strategy needed a drastic overhaul.

Serving More than One Market Segment

The HBA's mission is "leading the way to protect and promote housing and preserve the American dream of homeownership." It serves as a resource for consumers, housing policy makers, and the residential construction industry. Its website now reflects that triple mission, although

FIGURE 8.2 **Springfield HBA Home Page**
Springfield HBA revamped its website to effectively serve three different audiences. (Reprinted with permission from Springfield Home Builders Association, Springfield, Missouri)

balancing the needs of all three constituencies online has been a challenge. The association's web presence must simultaneously provide public information and insider or sensitive information for members only. Therefore, in redesigning its website, Greater Springfield distinguished the content visitors may view based on which user category the visitor is in.

Building by Blogging

In addition to segmenting content by user, Greater Springfield also recognized the need for all content to be current and relevant for members, policymakers, and consumers. Blogs were the association's solution for managing regular content updates with limited staffing. Blogs also provided a way to organize information by topic category. The HBA had 20 different blogs and nine locations where visitors went to blog. These blogs encompassed issues like advocacy by the HBA president and chief executive officer, and topics aimed at consumers like the local home shows and parades of homes, remodeling, and green building.

Texting to Twitter to Social Media Explosion

As recently as 2008 the HBA was not engaged in social media. That's when a new HBA board president, who habitually communicated by text message, took office. Morrow, who had never communicated by text message, picked up the routine when he began receiving text messages from his new board president. He discovered that text messaging was a natural, and often preferred, way for many builders and others in the construction industry to communicate. Active, busy, and rarely in front of a computer screen, home builders rely on their mobile phones. They want timely, concise information at their hip. This fact led Morrow to Twitter, the microblog with a 140-character limit for tweets. It was the first step toward Greater Springfield's comprehensive social media strategy, which includes the following elements:

Twitter. The association initially used Twitter to provide on-the-spot advocacy updates from the state capital, local courthouses, and other locations. HBA staff and senior leadership now routinely tweet useful, time sensitive, relevant information from HBA events and meetings to HBA members who follow them on Twitter. Busy HBA members can get basic news and links to more comprehensive detailed information and analysis of current housing issues, even if they can't attend every meeting. Twitter has become a powerful advocacy tool for the association. The HBA added a Twitter widget to the association's advocacy blog and encourages members to follow key Twitter streams. Twitter has been the key to syndicating all of the HBA's online content. All of the association's blogs tweet to an appropriate Twitter account and the blog and website pages display "Follow us on Twitter" links on each page. Blogs, syndicated news pages, and the HBA's meeting calendar automatically tweet new content to multiple sites and its Twitter followers. The list of followers includes consumers, who get tweets about shows and other opportunities that showcase HBA members and their products and services. Because of the volume of its tweets and followers, Greater Springfield uses tools, like SocialOomph, to program some tweets. These include promotional tweets about the local home show, such as reminders 20 minutes before every seminar or demonstration, with links to the HBA website and pages of additional information about the show.

Facebook. Although Twitter was a natural technology fit for the HBA, there was still a very important reason to actively engage on Facebook: its millions of users. Maintaining a meaningful Facebook presence while simultaneously managing a website and blogs is challenging but necessary because members and the public interact there. Although the association's RSS feed regularly updates the page, staff and members comment, share photos, and otherwise interact, which keeps the page fresh and authentic. Greater Springfield also buys targeted Facebook ads to promote local events. Even though people don't frequent Facebook to buy, they look to the social site for things to do.

YouTube. The association's YouTube channel is a vehicle for sharing and storing video content accumulated from its promotions, from local television news (with permission), and from members, that was taxing its local server's resources. These videos are easily embedded in blog posts, on the HBA's website, and in other content the association distributes.

E-newsletters. Although social media sites and users proliferate, many people still prefer e-mail communication. Programs like Constant Contact, iContact, and others facilitate subscription list management, design, and scheduling. To save money on postage, paper, printing, and hard copy design and composition, and to repurpose content, the HBA uses MailChimp to designate RSS feeds from its website to populate a regular weekly e-mail newsletter, *Housing News Weekly*. (The association replaced its monthly full-color newsletter with a quarterly.)

With all the consumer-focused content on Greater Springfield's website, the HBA also generates an e-newsletter for the general public. Transitioning from print to electronic communication saved $3,000 in production costs and generated new advertising revenue.

A Move-up Website

Morrow said, "The process of building and maintaining our website was like a very dysfunctional home-building process. We thought we had a pretty good idea of what we wanted when we began, but then we continually made slight modifications after the home's foundation was built.

When we were finished, we had a nice house. We were proud of it. But we also were acutely aware that this house—this labor of love—was built on a foundation intended for an entirely different house. We could live there for awhile, and even enjoy our stay. But we knew we would need to "move" soon or "rebuild" to have a fully-integrated, syndicated, and organized website as part of a comprehensive Internet Marketing strategy." Managing 20 blogs in 9 locations as well as several Twitter accounts, Facebook and LinkedIn pages and groups, a YouTube channel, weekly RSS-to-e-mail newsletters, and other social media became overwhelming. Following are a few of the goals the HBA compiled for a website redesign:

- Syndicate content to enable subscription-based RSS feeds, sub-feed categories.
- Add easily searchable archives with categories and subcategories.
- Fully integrate the website and website content with social media pages and HBA channels.
- Provide multiple access levels for subscribers to allow delivery of specialized content (public, member, committee chairs, board of directors, PAC board, etc.).
- Seamlessly push content to populate weekly e-mail newsletters for members and the public.
- Establish a website user interface to allow consumers to view content relevant and accessible to them but not anchor text that would prompt "access denied" messages.
- Install a content management system that would eliminate the need for a webmaster.
- Adopt a scalable design that would obviate the need for another costly overhaul in the short-term.

The new site is a sophisticated, multicategory, user friendly blog with RSS syndication, social media, video, and other features. A Find-a-Pro search tool enables consumer visitors to connect with builders, remodelers, and associates in the Greater Springfield area.

Attracting Visitors

Ceebraid Signal of Stamford, Connecticut, owns and manages apartment communities and other properties nationwide. When the company approached me in January 2009, the website for its six Connecticut apartment communities was built in Flash and had attracted fewer than 1,300 web visits for the entire month.

Although mRELEVANCE suggested migrating the website to PHP, the company wanted to maintain Flash programming for the website, even though it was a roadblock to SEO. To increase traffic and SEO, we built a new blog and began building links using some of our internal company websites and several key online directories.

By July 2009, traffic had increased by more than 60%, to more than 3,400 visits per month. With those results, we were able to convince the company that rebuilding the website in PHP and integrating a social media strategy would yield even greater returns. The new website, built in PHP with some Flash components, launched in February 2010 and has attracted an average of 7,000 visitors per month and a one-month high of 8,650. In addition, two of the company's properties have been sold to other investors, and three of the remaining six are almost fully leased.

Start Now

These case studies illustrate a common approach to creating an Internet marketing strategy: using both internal staff and outside consultants. Even if you prefer to do everything in-house, you should periodically ask an outside professional to review what you're doing and suggest ways to improve. If you follow the outline and concepts in this book, you will create a successful and profitable Internet marketing and social media program.

Although your company and brand are unique, each company should set benchmarks for Internet marketing and regularly review its strategy's effectiveness. Build your foundation with a search-engine-friendly website and blog. Make sure both sites address the five components of web development (content, navigation, design, functionality, and effectiveness). Create a holistic strategy. Determine your targeted keywords; develop a comprehensive social media program with a blog, microblogs, social networks, online PR, and social bookmark sites. Tie it all together with links so the various sites reinforce and update content on the others. This will save time and improve SEO. Most importantly, track your results every month so you can change and improve your strategy.

Whatever your current strategy is, you can probably be more efficient and effective at building on your competitive advantages and promoting your message online. Make sure you work with professional companies who can prove through tracking reports and SERPs that they will improve your SEO and Internet traffic. Building your program right will pay off with more visibility and more sales for your company.

You get what you pay for. It is never a good idea to leave your brand strategy and messaging to someone who does not understand your business, the technical details of available Internet marketing tools, and strategic marketing techniques. Your relative may be able to build a website and your college intern may be able to create a Facebook business page, but only a trained Internet marketing professional can integrate your program into a cohesive strategy to attract home buyers to your sales centers.

Endnotes

1 National Association of Realtors, *NAR Profile of Home Buyers and Sellers*, 2009, http://www.realtor.org/prodser.nsf/products/186-45-09?opendocument.

2 Jakob Nilsen, Alertbox website, http://www.useit.com/alertbox/reading_pattern.html, April 17, 2006.

3 EyeTools, *Eye Tracking Study*, http://eyetools.com/research_google_eyetracking_heatmap.html.

4 Carol Flammer, *Social Media for Homebuilders 2.0: It Is Easier Than You Think*, Washington, DC: NAHB BuilderBooks, 2011.

5 eMarketer, June 8, 2011, "Online Advertising Market Poised to Grow 20% in 2011," http://www.emarketer.com/PressRelease.aspx?R=1008432

6 Hitwise Monthly Category Report, June 2011, http://www.hitwise.com/us/press-center/industry-reports?j=13966109.

7 E-mail from Katie Curnutte, communications director, Zillow, 9/16/2011, based on actual August 2011 numbers.

8 Federal Trade Commission, CAN-SPAM Act: A Compliance Guide for Business, http://www.ftc.gov/bcp/edu/pubs/business/ecommerce/bus61.shtm.

Glossary

absolute unique visitor. The number of unduplicated visitors to your website within a specific period of time

absorption. The number of homes sold in a given market each month

Adwords. Google's pay-per-click program

algorithm. A series of mathematical calculations

ALT tag. The text that appears in a pop-up window when a visitor hovers his or her mouse pointer over an image. It describes the title of an image contained in the code for that image.

anchor text. Text that displays on a hyperlink

application programming interface (API). Routines and documentation that web developers use to integrate some applications into a website

average time on site. Amount of time a visitor spends on a website in any given session

banner ads. Graphics and images displayed to attract attention and prompt users to click on them

be-back. A return visitor to a sales center

black-hat SEO. Deliberate misrepresentation of the relevance of a website to the search engines designed to trick users into viewing pages that don't have the content they were looking for

blog categories. High-level topics into which blog content is organized

bookmark. A link a user saves in a browser to a site he or she plans to revisit

bots. Software applications built to travel from link to link on web sites to index every page on the Internet

bounce rate. Percentage of web visitors who visit only one web page during a session

bounced e-mail. E-mail not delivered to the recipient and returned to the sender

CAN-SPAM. A federal law that governs commercial e-mail

checkboxes. Data entry fields that allow you to select multiple options from a list

content management system (CMS). A web architecture for administering information on a site

cookie. A text file a web browser stores on a user's computer that allows a website to track information such as whether that computer has visited a site before

cost per click (CPC). *See* pay per click

cost per thousand (CPM). Cost per thousand, a method for pricing advertising based on the number of impressions or the number of times an ad will appear

direct traffic. Traffic that comes to a site from visitors typing a domain into the address bar of their web browser or selecting the address for it from a bookmark or a favorite they previously saved

domain name. The URL of a web page, such as www.BuilderBooks.com

DPI. Dots per inch. A measure of the resolution of photos and other images, or how finely they are recorded or displayed.

Drupal. An open-source PHP content management system

editorial calendar. Publishing schedule and topics for a blog

Extensible Markup Language (XML). The file type and data format for transferring listing data from a website database to an Internet advertising site that displays listing data and a file type for displaying data content on the Internet

favorite. A link to a frequently visited site a user can save in a browser, similar to a bookmark.

Firefox. A web browser, like Internet Explorer, that allows you to surf the Internet.

fixed marketing costs. Marketing costs that do not vary, such as market research and sales center rent.

footer file. A file that can be included on each page of a website that contains the information for the bottom section of the website

Friend. To add a person to your Facebook connections

Google Analytics. A software package that tracks key performance indicators and visitors on your website or blog

Google Places page. A business profile page that enables a company to share information about itself

Googlebot. Google's software "spider" that goes from web page to web page and to index a website

granular reporting. Detailed analysis of a traffic report using various criteria and time frames

hyperlink. Clickable text in a document or on a web page that takes a reader to another document or page location

HTML. Hyper text markup language. A website development language and a way to deliver graphic-intensive e-mail marketing messages.

impression. An appearance of an ad on a web page

intuitive. A descriptive term for a website that indicates the site has sensible navigation and is easy to use

Joomla. An open-source PHP content management system

JSP. Java server pages in an Internet programming language

key performance indicators (KPIs). Tracking metrics that demonstrate successful achievement of specific types of goals for specific activities

keyword. A word or phrase a user types into a search engine. Webmasters optimize websites for these keywords.

keyword density. The number of times a keyword or keyword phrase appears on a web page compared with the total number of words on the page. It is expressed as a percentage.

landing page. The first page a visitor sees when they click or type a URL

Like. An endorsement of your business page on Facebook

link juice. The relevance a link assigns a website for given anchor text

link titles. Metadata embedded in the code for a link that describes the title of a link

links. *See* hyperlinks

metadata. Code on a web page that describes the page

Millennials. Also called "Generation Y," these are people people born during the mid 1970s through the late 1990s.

navigation bar. A menu of links to pages on a website

no-follow tag. A metadata tag that tells the search engines not to follow a specific link

off-page SEO. SEO techniques used apart from the specific website or web page that is being optimized

online influencers. People who have social media accounts with many followers and who can reach many people

on-page SEO. SEO techniques used on a website or web page that is the focus of the optimization effort

open source. Software code available for anyone to modify and use

organic search results. Search engine results that appear because they are relevant to the search inquiry, not because they are paid ads.

page rank (PR). A link analysis algorithm that assigns numerical weight (PR score) to a web page and measures its relevance for a particular topic

pages per visit. The number of pages a visitor views when they go to a website

page view. One instance of a web page loaded by a browser

pay per click (PPC). A type of online advertising in which purchasers pay for an ad based on the number of times a user clicks it

PHP. A programming language used in website development

plug-in. Module of code that can be added to a blog to offer additional advanced functionality

pull-down choices. A data entry field for selecting one item in a list

radio button. A data entry field for selecting one item in a list

Really Simple Syndication (RSS). A means for automatically and electronically delivering content published on the web so it can be read, reused, and repurposed.

referring site traffic. Internet traffic that arrives at a site from inbound links on other websites or blogs

robots.txt file. A file on the server of your website that tells the search engines which pages to index and which pages to skip

RSS feed. A standardized mechanism for delivering published web content for repurposing or reuse

RSS feed reader. A website or application that enables a user to view the content of an RSS feed

Ruby on Rails. An open-source web application framework for programming a website

search engine marketing (SEM). Online marketing that relies on pay-per-click advertising

search engine optimization (SEO). The process of improving the visibility of a website or web page in search engines via natural or unpaid search results

search engine results page (SERP). A page that lists websites deemed relevant to a term a user types into a search engine

search engine traffic. Traffic from your SEO efforts and SEM traffic from your PPC campaigns

search volume. The number of searches for a given keyword in the search engines

session. A period of interaction between a browser and a website

site map. A file of all the pages on your website

social media optimization (SMO). The process of optimizing your social media profiles and sites for your particular keywords

spiders. Software applications built to travel from link to link on websites to index every page on the Internet

stickiness. A website's ability to hold visitors on the site for a long period of time

story board. A page-by-page representation of what a website or video will display

syndicate. The act of distributing online content

tags. Metadata specifically designed for SEO

teaser. A brief overview of content written to entice a visitor to a web page

title tag. Metadata that describes the title of a web page. The description appears at the top of the web browser window when the web page displays.

tracking report. A collection of data related to the visitors and their activity on a website

traffic sources. The external websites that link back to your website and drive traffic

tweet. A post on Twitter

usability. A web design concept that considers the location and organization of a site's navigation from a user's point of view

variable marketing costs. The portion of marketing and advertising budgets that may change month to month

visit. A period of interaction between a browser and a website

Web 2.0. Industry jargon that describes the Internet and how people build their websites, blogs, and social networking sites to encourage interaction and communication. Web 2.0 focuses conceptually on information sharing, collaboration, communication and interaction, and the social media concepts of user-generated content and virtual communities.

webmaster. A company or person that manages a website

white-hat SEO. SEO techniques that are generally accepted and proven effective over time

widget. A small software applet or module of functionality designed for a specific task

XML. *See* Extensible Markup Language

Resources

Unless otherwise noted, locate the following companies and products online by typing www.companyname (one word).com in your web browser.

Microblogs

Companies that create interactive floor plans:

- The BDX (http://www.thebdx.com/architectural-assets)
- Media Lab (http://www.medialab3dstudio.com/Architectural-Studio/Interactive-Ebrochure.htm)
- Floor Plan Online (http://floorplanonline.com/product-overview/interactive-floorplan-tours/)
- Maps Alive (http://www.mapsalive.com/Samples/)

Online Chat Software

You can read reviews of chat software at http://live-chat-support-software-review.toptenreviews.com/. My six favorites (in alphabetical order) are as follows:

- activSalesAgent
- Bold Chat
- Live Helper
- Live Person
- *PHP* Live
- Website Alive

Blog Plug-in

WordPress (http://wordpress.org/extend/plugins/)

Stock Photography Sites

- iStockphoto
- PunchStock
- Shutterstock

Microblogs

- Twitter
- FriendFeed
- Identi.ca
- Plurk
- Hometalk

Facebook Page Resources

- https://developers.facebook.com/blog/post/462/
- Facebook Places (http://www.facebook.com/facebookplaces)

Social Networking Sites

- Google+
- Facebook
- LinkedIn
- RealtyJoin
- ActiveRain
- Ning
- LiveJournal
- MySpace
- Wikipedia (http://en.wikipedia.org/wiki/List_of_social_networking_websites)

Local Search and Business Profile Sites

- Google Places (http://google.com/places/)
- Yahoo! Local (http://local.yahoo.com)

- Citysearch
- Yelp
- Facebook Places
- Foursquare
- Gowalla
- Better Business Bureau (http://www.bbb.org/online)
- Dogpile
- ZoomInfo

Public Relations Sites

- PRNewswire
- ClickPress
- PRZoom
- PRLog
- PRWeb

Photo and Video sites (with PR scores) as of this book's publication date:

- YouTube (9)
- Vimeo.com (9)
- Flickr (9)
- Picasa (8)
- Google Video (8)
- Dailymotion.com (8)
- MetaCafe.com (7)
- Lulu.com (7)
- Photobucket.com (7)
- Brightcove.com (6)
- BuzzNet.com (6)
- StupidVideos.com (6)
- Flixya (5)
- VMIX.com (5)

Social Bookmarking Sites

- Digg.com (http://digg.com)
- Delicious.com
- Reddit.com

- StumbleUpon.com
- Newsvine.com
- Mixx.com
- Propeller.com

Listing and Inventory Advertising Sites

- Realtor.com
- Trulia
- Zillow
- NewHomeSource.com
- NewHomesDirectory.com
- Craigslist (http://craigslist.org)
- Oodle.com
- Homes.com
- Backpage
- FrontDoor.com
- HotPads
- CLRSearch.com
- Enormo
- Propsmart
- BuilderPedia.com

Listing Tools

- Postlets.com
- RealBird.com
- Point2Builder.com
- Point2 Agent (http://agent.point2.com)

CRM and Lead Management Systems

- Pivotal (http://www.cdcsoftware.com/)
- Salesforce.com
- Sales Simplicity Software (http://salessimplicity.net)
- Builder1440
- BuildTopia
- CFT
- Lasso

- MARK System
- Sage ACT! (http://www.act.com)
- TopProducer

E-mail Marketing Programs

- Constant Contact
- Mail Chimp
- BuilderBrokerNews
- IContact

SEO Tools

- RankChecker by SEOBook (http://www.seobook.com)
- IBusinessPromoter.com
- FireFactor (http://www.coffeecup.com/firefactor/)
- SEOmoz (http://wwwseomoz.org)
- SearchEngineLand.com

Social Media Tracking Tools

- Radian6
- Alterian
- Jive Software
- Spiral16
- Klout

Index